CHAMBERS

Letter
Writing

مینیاتور
انتشارات

مرکز فروش کتاب های
آموزش زبان
مقدماتی تا عالی

ارچه کتاب،شماره ۷
٦٦٩٧٨٣٩٢-٣

425943

CHAMBERS
An imprint of Chambers Harrap Publishers Ltd
7 Hopetoun Crescent
Edinburgh EH7 4AY

This (second) edition published by Chambers Harrap Publishers Ltd 2005
Previous edition published as *Chambers Guide to Letter Writing* 1999
Copyright © Chambers Harrap Publishers Ltd 2005

We have made every effort to mark as such all words which we believe to
be trademarks. We should also like to make it clear that the presence of a
word in this book, whether marked or unmarked, in no way affects its
legal status as a trademark.

All rights reserved. No part of this publication may be reproduced, stored
in a retrieval system, or transmitted by any means, electronic, mechan-
ical, photocopying or otherwise, without the prior permission of the publisher.

A CIP catalogue record for this book is available from the British Library.

ISBN 0550 10141 1

808.
6
CHA

Designed and typeset by Chambers Harrap Publishers Ltd, Edinburgh
Printed and bound in Spain by Graphy Cems

CONTRIBUTORS

Editors
Kay Cullen
Elaine O'Donoghue

Series Editor
Elaine O'Donoghue

Publishing Manager
Patrick White

Prepress Manager
Sharon McTeir

Prepress Controller
Claire Williamson

Letter Writing ، لیتوگرافی: فرااندیش، چاپ: گوهر اندیشه، چاپ اول: بهار ۱۳۸۵، تیراژ: ۳۰۰۰ نسخه، ناشر: تک‌نواز، مرکز پخش: انتشارات رهنما، مقابل دانشگاه تهـران، خیابان فروردیـن، نبش خیابان شهـدای ژاندارمـری، پلاک ۲۲۰، تلفن: ۶۶۴۰۰۹۲۷ ،۶۶۴۱۶۶۰۴- فاکس: ۶۶۴۶۸۱۹۴ ، فروشگاه رهنما، سعادت‌آباد، خیابان علامه طباطبایی جنوبی، پلاک ۸ تلفن: ۸۸۶۹۴۱۰۲ ، تلفن فروشگاه شماره ۴: ۶۶۴۱۶۴۳۲ ، نمایشگاه کتاب رهنما، مقابل دانشگاه تهران پاسـاژ فروزنده، تلفن: ۶۶۹۵۰۹۵۷

CONTENTS

Introduction

Letter writing is the only device for combining solitude with good company.

Lord Byron

There is nothing to compare with the pleasure of receiving a personal letter, be it a message of support, a handwritten thank-you card or a chatty letter filled with news. Letters can be kept and read again and again. For centuries, letters have fanned the flames of romance – or extinguished them; have sustained friendships across the miles; have been the conduits for diplomacy and politics; and have spread knowledge and news around the world. Much of what we know of the past has been gleaned from letters.

Letters have not lost relevance in the present. For many people, letters are still the most acceptable medium for business correspondence, for applying for jobs, for writing to newspapers and for making complaints. However, in this technological age email and, to a lesser extent, fax have introduced new areas of written communication, bringing with them new sets of conventions and style. This book is an essential guide to all these forms of communication.

Part 1 deals with preparation for letter writing: deciding on the tone, the style and the layout of the correspondence. Part 2 considers specific forms such as business letters, CVs and applications, and letters of complaint. Part 3 is dedicated to the ever-expanding area of e-mail correspondence. The extensive supplement contains helpful tips for writing on-screen, and gives guidance on grammar, style and punctuation with the aid of numerous examples. The symbol ✔ before an example is the indicator of correct use, and the symbol ✗ identifies examples that are incorrect.

Useful phrases, as well as sample letters, CVs and cards, are provided throughout. Although they contain many standard phrases that can be put to good use in specific contexts, these models are intended as a guide only, and should not be copied exactly. Adapt the material to suit your style and tone and make the letters more personal.

A good dictionary, such as *The Chambers Dictionary*, can help with spelling and accuracy of meaning, while *The Chambers Thesaurus* can enrich vocabulary and add variety and spice to your letters.

Other Desktop Guides are: *Perfect Punctuation*, *Common Errors* and *Effective Grammar*. The *Chambers Good Writing Guide* provides useful tips on a wide variety of relevant topics including style, sensitive language and proofreading your own work.

Part One

General Guidelines

Planning a letter

Although it is no longer the fastest or necessarily the most convenient way of communicating, there are still many occasions when writing a letter is preferable to using the telephone or sending an e-mail or text message:

- Sometimes letters are written so that everyone who is involved understands exactly what is being discussed or agreed upon. It is often important to have a written record of decisions or transactions.
- There are still some people – albeit fewer and fewer every year – who do not have access to e-mail, and a letter may be the only way of sending a written message to them.
- Sometimes the time and effort spent writing a letter is an expression of the personal relationship you have with someone.

The first of these reasons generally relates to formal letters and business letters, and the second and third relate to informal and personal letters. These kinds of letter tend to be written in different styles.

It is always important to plan your letter. To focus your mind, before starting to write any letter, ask yourself the following questions:

- **What** am I writing? Are you producing a particular kind of document that needs to conform to a certain format or style such as a formal or business letter?
- **Who** am I writing this for? Will the person who is going to read this expect it to be presented in formal or informal language? Will they be familiar with all of the technical terms

3

that you might wish to use? What do they need to know that they might not know already?

- **Why** am I writing it? Do you want to provide information, argue a point of view, ask for advice, make a complaint or give instructions? Do you have a single intention or several different intentions? Whatever the case, it is best to be clear from the start about what you are setting out to do.
- **What** response do I want? Do you want to receive an acknow-ledgement, a specific piece of information, or an apology from the person to whom you are writing? Do you need to make this clear in what you write?
- **How** am I going to present it? Once you know what you are writing and why you are writing it, you should be able to form some ideas about the type of language you need to use and your manner of presentation. For example, is a lengthy explanation required, or will a quick summary be sufficient? Do you want to present information using lists with bullet points?

The aim of a letter is to communicate effectively. As with any piece of writing, think about what you are trying to achieve and the best way to do this:

- **Structure**: make sure that your letter has a clear and coherent structure so that the reader can easily follow the points made and knows what action, if any, is required or expected.
- **Tone**: think about the tone you wish to create. Do you want to appear impersonal and businesslike, or is a more familiar tone called for?
- **Style**: aim for a direct, easy-to-read style, even in formal letters. Match your style to the type of letter you are writing. Avoid being long-winded or pompous when writing formal letters.
- **Punctuation**: create an uncluttered, more open feel to your writing by using punctuation only to avoid ambiguity or to allow the reader to pause in a long sentence.

Formal letters

Formal letters are written to, for example, your local councillor, your member of parliament or a prospective employer.

The formal letters written by private individuals on social and personal matters are similar in layout to the business letters sent out by commercial companies and other organizations. However, business letters are only one type of formal letter, and they tend to be more heavily structured, with various conventional forms that are not required in other types of formal letter. If you are writing a formal, non-business letter avoid using the conventional abbreviations found in business letters, such as 'Enc' for 'enclosure' and 'cc' for 'copied to'. The person you are writing to may not be familiar with these abbreviations. Write out such points within the letter itself, ie 'I enclose ...', and 'I am sending a copy of this letter to ... .

Business letters are discussed in detail in Part 2.

Organizing and structuring the content of a formal letter

Always be polite and succinct. Make it easy for your reader to extract the point you are trying to make.

1. It is a good idea to begin your letter with a short **introductory paragraph**, which may be used to acknowledge any previous letter you have received and to state the subject of your letter.
2. You can follow this with the **development**: a longer paragraph or series of paragraphs expanding the various points you want to make in a logical sequence and providing relevant details where required.
3. End with a short final paragraph (the **conclusion**), summarizing the main points or outlining any action or recommendations.

For examples of formal letters on various subjects see Part 2.

Informal letters

When writing to friends and relatives you can write in any way you like, using a relaxed, conversational style. Informal letters may be more loosely structured than formal letters. The letter may be handwritten or typed. People whose handwriting is very difficult to read should consider using a computer or typewriter. To help a reader with poor eyesight, use black or dark blue ink on white paper to give good contrast or use a larger font size in your word-processing package.

Checking your letter

Once you have finished writing your letter, you need to look over it again to make sure everything is in order before you send it off to the person or people who will read it. It is important that it is clear, achieves the right tone, and is free from errors.

Looking at your letter on paper

If you are writing on-screen it is important to look at your letter on paper once it is finished to make sure it looks and reads as you intended. Fonts, font sizes, headings, spaces and blocks of text all may look different on the printed page than on the screen. Looking at a printout is particularly important to check that the text of the letter is balanced and fills up the entire page, rather than being squashed into the top half.

Reading through your letter

It is a good idea to read through your letter at least twice. The first time you read through what you have written you can skim through it quickly to make sure it is properly organized and conveys what you wanted to say. When have done this, you can proofread it to check for spelling mistakes and inconsistencies in grammar or punctuation.

The spellcheck function on your computer may help to identify some keying errors and simple spelling mistakes. However, it will not pick up cases of a correctly spelled word being inappropriately used.

For this reason, you should always read your finished document carefully yourself.

- It is advisable to take a break between the end of the writing process and the start of the proofreading process so that you can give your eyes and brain a rest.
- When you proofread, you read through a text with the sole intention of checking spelling, punctuation and grammar, and alphabetical and numerical order. At this stage you should not be thinking about whether the information is factually accurate or clearly expressed.
- Do not assume that a document will be correct, and actively focus on looking for mistakes. You need to be especially alert and critical.
- If it is an important letter or a document such as a CV, ask someone else to proofread it as well. A fresh pair of eyes will often see things that you miss.

Layout of letters

Now that you have decided on what you have to say, it is time to consider setting the letter out on the page.

Standard parts of a letter

A formal letter contains six standard parts:

- Your name, address and contact details (see below).
- The name and address of the person or organization you are writing to. If you are writing to a specific person, include their title or position.
- The date (see below).
- A greeting or salutation. The form this takes depends on how well you know the correspondent. The conventions of greetings are discussed on pages 17–20.
- A heading that will help the recipient to see at a glance what your letter is about. The heading should follow the opening greeting and be typed or written on a new line with at least one line space above and below it. The heading in a typed or hand-written letter is usually underlined or typed/printed entirely in capital letters to make it stand out. If you are using a computer you have the option of using bold type or a larger font size for the heading.
- The main part of the letter.
- The ending or complimentary close. Like the greeting, this follows certain conventions in a formal letter (see pages 18–20).

Business letters are discussed in detail in Part 2.

An informal letter can take any form you like. Most people include their own address and the date, but it is not necessary to include your correspondent's contact details and rare to include a heading.

Presenting your letter

It is important to pay attention to how your letter appears. A neat, well-laid-out letter will not only make a good impression, but is a courtesy to the person you are writing to. This is important for letters generally, and for job applications and other formal letters in particular:

Ink

- Unless you are corresponding with a close friend or relative, use dark blue or black ink – even if you are just signing a letter that has been typed. Avoid thick marker pens, coloured ink (other than blue or black) and pencil.
- If typing your letter on a typewriter, make sure the ribbon or ink cartridge in your machine will produce clear and even print. Similarly, when printing letters written on-screen, ensure that the paper is clean and that the printer has not smudged the text.

Paper

- The best advice is to stick to plain white or cream for business, official and more formal types of personal correspondence. For informal letters to friends or family, you can choose any type of paper. (For more information on paper, see Supplement.)
- When applying for a job, use identical stationery – preferably good-quality white paper – for the covering letter and CV.
- For personal and less formal letters, you can write on both sides of the sheet. If your handwritten letter stretches to more than three sides, it is a good idea to number the second and subsequent sheets.
- Business and official letters should be typed or written on one

side only, using continuation sheets for the second and subsequent pages.

- Unlined paper should always be used for typed correspondence and is also recommended for handwritten letters. If you find it difficult to write by hand in evenly-spaced horizontal lines, use a guide sheet (usually supplied with the pad) ruled up with heavy black lines under the sheet you are writing on.

Spacing

- Divide information logically into clearly identifiable paragraphs, even if these are only one sentence long.
- Use a two-line space between paragraphs or individual lines if this will improve the general appearance.
- It is important to achieve a good balance between the size of the sheet of paper and what is to be written on it. If the letter is short, the text should not be pushed up to the top of the sheet with a large area left blank at the bottom – leave some space at the top to balance that at the bottom of the sheet.
- If the letter is long, it will detract from the overall appearance if the first sheet is closely spaced, and only one or two short lines go over on to the second sheet. Try to space the letter more generously, so that more text appears on the second sheet.

Remember that a draft will make it easier to refine and correct the content before you begin to write or type your letter. The final letter, whether it is handwritten or typed, should be free of corrections and errors.

> **i**
>
> When writing on-screen, note that many word-processing programs have tools that provide useful templates for laying out and formatting various types of letters.

Blocked and indented styles

Letters can be presented in one of two styles: **blocked style** or **indented style**. Nowadays, the majority of business letters and most other typed letters are in **blocked style**. The **indented style**, also known as **semi-blocked**, is a more traditional format and is now rarely used for business letters. However, some people still prefer the indented style for both formal and informal letters, especially those that are handwritten.

Blocked style

In a fully blocked letter the following conventions apply:

- All paragraphs and headings are set against the left-hand margin if headed paper, which contains the sender's address, is being used (see below).
- If headed paper is not used, the sender's address and the date are set on the right-hand side of the page, although they are still aligned to the left (each line begins directly underneath the previous line).
- Underneath the sender's address and the date, but on the left-hand side of the page, comes the address of the person to whom the letter is being sent.
- Each new line and each new paragraph is set against the margin of the page, rather than being moved in slightly or 'indented'.
- At least one line of clear space is inserted between each paragraph, and between every other separate element of the letter.
- In keeping with modern English usage, a minimal style of punctuation is adopted; thus no commas are used in the address, date, or opening and closing lines of the letter.
- Full stops are not generally used for abbreviations.

LETTER IN BLOCKED STYLE (formal letter)

89 Buchanan Street
Canterbury
Kent
CT1 3QE

4 June 2005

The Manager
Shipton's Bank
201 Cornmarket Street
Canterbury
Kent
CT2 4XD

Dear Sir

Account No. 32132138

This is to confirm my telephone call to your branch this
morning asking you to stop payment of cheque number
10456 issued by me to Fargo & Sons, written for the
sum of £780 and dated 27 May 2005.

I would be grateful if you could confirm that the original
cheque has been stopped, so that I may issue a new one.

I look forward to hearing from you.

Yours faithfully

Robert Clark

Robert Clark

Indented style

For more informal letters, including those that are handwritten, the format most widely used is known as **indented** or **semi-blocked**.

In an indented letter:

- The sender's address is typed or written on the right-hand side of the sheet but with the second and subsequent lines of the address beginning one or two characters to the right of the first letter of the preceding line.
- The recipient's address is not usually written. If it is included, it is aligned to the left of the sheet as for blocked style.
- The salutation is aligned to the left-hand margin, but all other first lines are usually indented.
- Any heading following the salutation is centred above the main text of the letter.
- Because the indenting shows where paragraphs begin and end, there are not usually clear lines between paragraphs. However, you can also include clear lines if you wish.
- The complimentary close can be indented from the left margin, centred under the main text or (in some formal typed letters) placed near the right-hand margin of the sheet.
- Commas can be included in the date and after the opening and close.
- Full stops can be used for abbreviations.

LETTER IN INDENTED STYLE (informal letter)

40, Crescent Lane
Weston
Bath
BA2 5DS

9th February 2005

Dear Anne,

Thank you for your letter and the photos. It was so nice to hear your news and see the pictures. I'm glad that you're all well and that the party went well. I wish I could have been there.

I'm sorry I haven't written for so long. Life has been very hectic of late and it's not getting any quieter! Not that I'm complaining... We are both working very hard and looking forward to a break at the end of the month, maybe a week skiing in Italy.

Fred sends his best to all of you. We both hope to see you very soon. How about a weekend visit in April?

Give my love to all the family. Write soon.

Love

Melanie
XXX

PS I love the photo of you dancing on the table!

Contact details

It is important to provide contact details so that your correspondent can reply to you quickly and easily. The information you provide will vary depending on whether the letter is formal or informal, and whether you use headed paper or not. Some people use their own pre-printed adhesive address labels and these can be affixed to the top right-hand corner of the letter.

Headed paper

An official letter or a business letter is almost always written on the firm's or organization's headed notepaper. The name, address, telephone number, etc printed at the top of the page is known as the **letterhead**. If the firm or organization has a logo this will be printed as part of the letterhead.

Non-headed paper

After your address you may wish to include your telephone number and other contact details:

- Make it clear to the reader what the number refers to by writing *Tel:* or *Phone:* in front of it.
- You might also include a mobile phone number on a separate line. Indicate that this is not a land line by writing *Mobile:* in front of it.
- Indicate an extension number by the letters *Ext.*
- Place your regional code in brackets, or put a dash between the regional code and your personal number.
- You may also wish to give your fax number (*Fax:*), e-mail address (*E-mail:*) and website address (*Web:*).

Date

No punctuation is required in the date when it is written in the order day (in figures), followed by month (written out in full), followed by year (in figures):

29 November 2005

American style is as follows:

November 29, 2005

> **Usage**
>
> Nowadays, it is less common to write dates using ordinal numbers, such as 29th November 2005.

If you choose to include the name of the day as well as its number, it is usual to insert a comma between the name and number:

Tuesday, 29 November 2005

Other styles used in writing dates do have punctuation of one sort or another. There may be hyphens between the elements, as in:

29-Nov-2005

Or slashes between the elements, as in:

29/11/05
29/11/2005

Or stops between one or more of the elements, as in:

29.11.2005

i

Remember that in the USA (and in countries that have adopted the US system) 12/7/2006 means **7 December 2006**, while in the UK it means **12 July 2006**.

Beginnings, endings and correct forms of address

There are many conventions for opening and closing letters, depending on the type of letter, the relationship between the writer and recipient and the position of the recipient. This chapter looks in detail at these topics. E-mails have slightly different conventions and are dealt with in Part 3.

The opening greeting or salutation

The beginning of a letter, where you address yourself to your correspondent, is called an **opening greeting** or **salutation**:

- In business letters, the usual opening greeting should begin with 'Dear'. The greeting takes various forms, depending on whether or not you know the name of the individual to whom you are writing.
- If you can, address the person by name (*Dear Dr Steadman*). You can often find out the name and correct job title of the person with whom you wish to correspond by contacting a company or organization by phone or by checking their website.
- If you do not know the name of the person or are not confident about the correct style of address, use *Dear Sir*, *Dear Madam* or *Dear Sir/Madam*.
- Remember that people can be sensitive about having their name written incorrectly. You want to avoid getting off to a bad start, so take care to get the name and style of address correct. Watch out for unorthodox spellings and for people who are styled *Dr*, *Lord*, *Lady*, etc rather than *Mr* or *Ms*.
- Correct forms of address for people of rank and title are dealt with later in this chapter.
- The opening greeting for informal letters can be in any form you think appropriate.

- In American punctuation, full stops are more commonly used after abbreviations such as *Mr.*, *Dr.* and *Ms.*

The complimentary close

The ending of a letter where you 'sign off' is known as the **complimentary close**. The wording of the salutation at the beginning of the letter determines the wording of the complimentary close:

- For business and formal letters, use the form of the complimentary close that matches the opening greeting (see below).
- In formal letters, no commas are needed after the complimentary close.
- For a business letter and other formal letters where you are known to your correspondent, the complimentary close used may be less formal.
- In informal letters, you can use any close you wish.
- In American usage, the complimentary closes used are different from those used in British usage.

When you don't know the name of the person to whom you are writing:		
	GREETING	**CLOSE**
	Dear Sir	Yours faithfully
	Dear Madam	Faithfully yours (*US*)
	Dear Sir or Madam	
	Dear Sir/Madam	
Writing to a company, newspaper or organization:	Dear Sirs (*Br*)	
	Gentlemen (*US*)	

Usage

Never use 'Yours very faithfully'.

When you know the name of the person to whom you are writing:

GREETING	CLOSE
Dear Mr Jameson	Yours sincerely (*Br*)
Dear Mrs Lucas	Sincerely yours (*US*)
Dear Ms Green	Sincerely (*US*)
Dear Dr Illingworth	

More friendly tone: Yours very sincerely (*Br*)

Less formal: With best wishes
With best regards
Kindest regards

Less frequently: Yours respectfully (*Br*)
Respectfully yours (*US*)
Respectfully

Usage

As a useful aid to remembering which greeting and close to use for formal letters, try the following: *Sir* and *sincerely* don't go together.

When writing to a friend or relative:		
	GREETING	**CLOSE**
When writing to a friend or relative:	Dear Bill Dear Asif Dear Mum and Dad	With love Love Love and best wishes
Less formal:	Hi John! Hello there	
More affectionate:	Dearest/My dearest Jill	With all my love Much love Lots of love
More formal:		Yours All the best Best wishes
Familiar:		See you soon Cheers (*Br*) Bye for now

Correct forms of address

You may have to write to someone who holds an official title or rank, such as a member of the clergy or a peer of the realm. The correct forms to use in the address and opening greeting are shown below.

Ambassador

○ **Address on letter and envelope:** HE Mr [forename] [surname]
○ **Open letter with:** Dear Ambassador
○ **Close letter with:** Yours faithfully

Archbishop (Anglican)

- Address on letter and envelope: The Most Reverend the Archbishop of —
- Open letter with: My Lord Archbishop
- Close letter with: Yours faithfully

Archbishop (of Canterbury and York)

- Address on letter and envelope: The Most Reverend and Rt Hon The Lord Archbishop of —
- Open letter with: My Lord Archbishop
- Close letter with: Yours faithfully

Archbishop (Catholic)

- Address on letter and envelope: His Grace the Archbishop of —
- Open letter with: My Lord Archbishop or (less formally) Dear Archbishop
- Close letter with: Yours faithfully

Baron

- Address on letter and envelope: The Rt Hon Lord [surname]
- Open letter with: My Lord or (less formally) Dear Lord [surname]

i

In countries such as Germany, Sweden and the Baltic states the title of Baron is never translated as 'Lord'. Baron von Richthofen is addressed as such, and not as 'Lord von Richthofen'.

Baroness (wife of baron)

- Address on letter and envelope: The Rt Hon Lady [surname]
- Open letter with: Dear Madam or (less formally) Dear Lady [surname]

Baroness (in own right)

- Address on letter and envelope: The Rt Hon Lady [surname] or The Rt Hon the Baroness [surname]
- Open letter with: Dear Madam or (less formally) Dear Lady [surname]

Baronet

- Address on letter and envelope: Sir [forename] [surname], Bt
- Open letter with: Dear Sir or (less formally) Dear Sir [forename]

Baronet's wife

- Address on letter and envelope: Lady [surname]
- Open letter with: Dear Madam or (less formally) Dear Lady [surname]

Bishop (Anglican)

- Address on letter and envelope: The Right Reverend The Lord Bishop of —
- Open letter with: My Lord Bishop or My Lord
- Close letter with: Yours faithfully

Bishop (Roman Catholic)

- Address on letter and envelope: His Lordship the Bishop of —
- Open letter with: My Lord
- Close letter with: Yours faithfully

Bishop (Orthodox)

- Address on letter and envelope: The Right Reverend Bishop of —
- Open letter with: Your Grace
- Close letter with: Yours faithfully

Cabinet Members

- Address on letter and envelope: The Rt Hon [title] eg The Rt Hon The Secretary of State for Foreign and Commonwealth Affairs
- Open letter with: Dear [title] eg Dear Foreign Secretary

Cardinal

- Address on letter and envelope: His Eminence Cardinal [surname]
- Open letter with: Your Eminence
- Close letter with: Yours faithfully

Chief Rabbi

- Address on letter and envelope: The Very Reverend the Chief Rabbi
- Open letter with: Dear Chief Rabbi or Dear Sir
- Close letter with: Yours faithfully

Christian Clergy (Anglican and Protestant Churches)

- Address on letter and envelope: The Reverend [forename] [surname]
- Open letter with: Dear Sir/Madam or Dear Mr/Mrs/Miss/Ms [surname]

Christian Clergy (Roman Catholic)

- Address on letter and envelope: The Reverend [forename] [surname] (If a member of a religious order, the initials of the order should follow the name)
- Open letter with: Dear Reverend Father

Councillor

- Address on letter and envelope: (for a man) Councillor [forename] [surname]; (for a woman) Councillor Mrs/Miss/Ms [forename] [surname]
- Open letter with: Dear Councillor [surname]; Dear Councillor Mrs/Miss/Ms [surname] or Dear Mr/Mrs/Miss/Ms

Countess

- Address on letter and envelope: The Rt Hon the Countess of —
- Open letter with: Madam or (less formally) Dear Lady —

Courtesy titles

When a peer holds other titles, by courtesy one of the lesser ones is used by his heir.

The remaining children of a duke or marquess:

- Address on letter and envelope: Lord/Lady [forename] [surname]
- Open letter with: My Lord/Dear Madam or (less formally) Dear Lord/Lady [forename]

The sons and daughters of earls:

○ Address on letter and envelope: The Honourable/Lady [forename] [surname]

○ Open letter with: Dear Mr [surname]/Lady [forename]

The children of viscounts, barons and life peers who have no courtesy title

○ Address on letter and envelope: The Honourable [forename] [surname]

○ Open letter with: Dear Mr/Miss [surname]

Dame

○ Address on letter and envelope: Dame [forename] [surname] (followed by letters of the order)

○ Open letter with: Dear Madam *or* (less formally) Dear Dame [forename]

Doctor (of medicine)

○ Address on letter and envelope: Doctor *or* Dr [forename] [surname]

○ Open letter with: Dear Doctor *or* Dr [surname]

➤ See also **Surgeon**

Doctorate, holder of

○ Address on letter and envelope: the initials DD, LLD, MD, MusD, etc may be placed after the ordinary form of address

○ Open letter with: Dear Sir/Madam *or* Dear Dr [surname]

i

Right Honourable (Rt Hon) is used by Baron, Earl, Lord Mayor, Lord Provost, Privy Counsellor, Viscount and equivalent female ranks.

Duchess

○ Address on letter and envelope: Her Grace the Duchess of —

○ Open letter with: Dear Madam *or* (less formally) Dear Duchess

Duke

○ Address on letter and envelope: His Grace the Duke of —

○ Open letter with: My Lord Duke *or* (less formally) Dear Duke

Earl

- Address on letter and envelope: His Rt Hon the Earl of —
- Open letter with: My Lord or (less formally) Dear Lord —

First Minister (Scotland and Northern Ireland)

- Address on letter and envelope: [The Rt Hon] the First Minister
- Open letter with: Dear First Minister

First Secretary (Wales)

- Address on letter and envelope: [The Rt Hon] the First Secretary
- Open letter with: Dear First Secretary

Governor (US)

- Address on letter and envelope: The Honorable [forename] [surname] Governor of [state]
- Open letter with: Dear Governor [surname]

Judge (High Court)

- Address on letter and envelope: The Rt Hon Mr/Mrs Justice [surname] (note that Mrs is used even to an unmarried woman)
- Open letter with: Dear Sir/Madam or (less formally) Dear Judge

Judge (Circuit)

- Address on letter and envelope: His/Her Honour Judge [surname] QC (if appropriate)
- Open letter with: Dear Sir/Madam or (less formally) Dear Judge

Junior Minister

- Address on letter and envelope: [forename] [surname] MP Minister of State, [department]
- Open letter with: Dear Minister

Knight

- Address on letter and envelope: Sir [forename] [surname] followed by the initials of the order, eg KCB (of the Bath), KCMG (of St Michael and St George), KG (of the Garter), KT (of the Thistle)
- Open letter with: Dear Sir [forename] or according to person's rank

Lady

- Address on letter and envelope: Lady [surname]
- Open letter with: Dear Lady [surname]

Life Peer

- Address on letter and envelope: The Rt Hon the Lord [surname]
- Open letter with: My Lord or (less formally) Dear Lord [surname] (note that the full title, eg *Lord Holden of Hazeldean*, should not be used on letters. Use only *Lord Holden*)

Life Peeress

- Address on letter and envelope: The Rt Hon the Baroness [surname] or The Rt Hon the Lady [surname]
- Open letter with: My Lady or (less formally) Dear Lady [surname] (as with a life peer use only the title and surname in the address)

Marchioness

- Address on letter and envelope: The Most Hon the Marchioness of —
- Open letter with: Dear Lady —

Marquess

- Address on letter and envelope: The Most Hon the Marquess of —
- Open letter with: Dear Lord —

Mayor

UK and Ireland

Lord Mayor

- Address on letter and envelope: The Lord Mayor of [town or city] (whether male or female)
- Open letter with: Dear Lord Mayor

Lord Mayor of London, Cardiff, York, Dublin and Belfast

- Address on letter and envelope: The Rt Hon the Lord Mayor of [town or city] (whether male or female)

- Open letter with: My Lord Mayor or (less formally) Dear Lord Mayor

Lord Provosts of Edinburgh, Glasgow, Aberdeen and Dundee

- Address on letter and envelope: The Rt Hon the Lord Provost of the City of —
- Open letter with: Dear Lord Provost

Mayors of cities and boroughs

- Address on letter and envelope: The Mayor of [town or city] (whether male or female)
- Open letter with: Dear Mr Mayor (whether male or female)

United States

- Address: The Honorable (full name), Mayor of (city)
- Begin letter: Dear Sir/Madam or Dear Mr/Madam Mayor

Member of Parliament

- Address on letter and envelope: the usual form of address, followed by MP, MSP, AM, MLA and MEP for a member of the UK Parliament, Scottish Parliament, National Assembly for Wales, Northern Ireland Assembly and European Parliament respectively.
- Open letter with: Dear Mr/Mrs/Miss/Ms [surname]

> **Usage**
>
> Note that MP/MSP etc comes *after* any honours and decorations, eg Mr John McDougal OBE, MP

Officers (serving in the Armed Forces)

- Address on letter and envelope: The professional rank precedes any other rank or title.
- Open letter with: Dear [rank] [surname]

Officers (retired)

- Naval officers above the rank of Lieutenant, army officers above the rank of Captain, and air force officers above the rank of

Flight Lieutenant may continue to use and be addressed by their armed forces rank after being placed on the retired list

Pope

- Address on letter and envelope: His Holiness the Pope
- Open letter with: Your Holiness or Most Holy Father
- Close letter with: (for Roman Catholics) I have the honour to be, your Holiness's most humble (or devoted and obedient) child; (non-Catholics) I have the honour to be (or remain), Your Holiness's obedient servant

President of the United States

- Address on letter and envelope: The President
- Open letter with: Sir/Madam or Dear Mr/Madam President
- Close letter with: Yours sincerely

Prime Minister

- Address on letter and envelope: The Rt Hon The Prime Minister
- Open letter with: Dear Sir/Madam or (less formally) Dear Prime Minister (or address according to any other rank held that takes precedence)

> **Usage**
>
> For royalty, it is more usual to address any correspondence to a private secretary, equerry or lady-in-waiting, by title but not by name. Subsequent correspondence should be sent to the actual writer of the reply.

Prince

- Address on letter and envelope: (if a duke) His Royal Highness the Duke of —; (if the son of the sovereign, but not a duke) His Highness, the Prince [forename]; (otherwise) His Royal Highness Prince [forename]
- Open letter with: Sir
- Close letter with: I have the honour to be (or remain), Sir, Your Royal Highness's humble and obedient servant

Princess

- Address on letter and envelope: (if a duchess) Her Royal Highness the Duchess of —; (if the daughter of the sovereign, but not a duchess) Her Royal Highness, the Princess [forename]; (if a princess by marriage) HRH Princess [husband's forename] of —; (otherwise) Her Royal Highness Princess [forename]
- Open letter with: Madam
- Close letter with: I have the honour to be (or remain), Madam, Your Royal Highness's humble and obedient servant

Professor

- Address on letter and envelope: Professor [forename] [surname]
- Open letter with: Dear Sir/Madam

Queen

- Address on letter and envelope: Her Majesty the Queen or The Private Secretary to Her Majesty the Queen
- Open letter with: Madam
- Close letter with: I have the honour to be (or remain), Madam, Your Majesty's most humble and obedient servant

Representative (US Federal)

- Address on letter and envelope: The Honorable [forename] [surname]
- Open letter with: Sir/Madam or Dear Congressman/Congresswoman [surname]

Senator (Federal)

- Address on letter and envelope: The Honorable [forename] [surname]
- Open letter with: Sir/Madam or Dear Senator [surname]

Surgeon

- Address on letter and envelope: Mr/Mrs/Miss/Ms [forename] [surname]
- Open letter with: Dear Mr/Mrs/Miss/Ms [surname]

> *Usage*
>
> In England and Wales, obstetricians and gynaecologists are addressed as for a surgeon; in Scotland, Ireland and elsewhere as for a doctor of medicine.

Vice President of the United States

○ Address on letter and envelope: The Vice President
○ Open letter with: Sir/Madam *or* Dear Mr/Madam Vice President

Viscount

○ Address on letter and envelope: The Rt Hon the Viscount —
○ Open letter with: My Lord *or* (less formally) Dear Lord —

Viscountess

○ Address on letter and envelope: The Rt Hon the Viscountess —
○ Open letter with: Madam *or* (less formally) Dear Lady —

Useful sources

For more extensive information about the correct forms of address, see the Department for Constitutional Affairs website:

http://www.dca.gov.uk/dept/titles.htm

Addresses and sending letters to other countries

Addressing the envelope

The address should be parallel to the longer sides of the envelope. It should be positioned slightly to the left of the mid-point between the two shortest sides, with the first line of the address about two-thirds of the way down from the top edge of the envelope. This allows plenty of room for the stamp and postmark.

When you write the address:

- Use ink that is clearly legible, avoiding light colours such as yellow or white.
- If typing the address, ensure that the font is between 10 and 12 point.
- Include the name and title of the recipient.
- Include the separate elements of the address on separate lines.
- The postcode should always be in upper case, without punctuation.
- There should be no inverted commas around a house name.
- You can abbreviate words such as *Road* and *Street* to *Rd* and *St* even in formal letters (see list at the end of this chapter).
- No commas are needed to mark the separate parts of the address in formal letters and are not obligatory in indented style.
- Initialisms (eg *UK*, *USA*) should have no full stops.
- In indented style, full stops may be used after abbreviations of customary titles (eg *Dr.*, *Mrs.*, *Mr.*), street names (eg *Rd.*, *St.*, *Ave.*), or after the type of abbreviation that does not include the first and last letter of the full form (eg *Prof.*, *The Rev.*, *Lancs.*, *Bucks.*) or, equally correctly, may be omitted.

- If you are using an envelope with a window (see page 178), make sure that the entire address is clearly visible through the window.

> **Usage**
>
> So that the letter can be scanned and sorted electronically, postal services prefer that no punctuation or underlining be used in the name and address on the envelope, particularly in any postcodes. They also advise that there should be a clear zone of 5mm around the address.

Sender's address on the envelope

Many businesses use address labels with their own name and address printed along the top or bottom edge, or use envelopes printed with their logo and address. This helps the post office if the letter or package has to be returned to the sender for any reason. If you are concerned that your letter may not reach its destination, or that the post office will not be able to deliver it, you should write or print your own name and address on the back of the envelope, making it clear that you are the sender.

> **Usage**
>
> In most EU countries the sender's address is usually written on the back of the envelope. In North America, the sender's address is usually written on the upper left-hand corner of the front of the envelope.

Stamps

Postage stamps should be affixed to the top right-hand corner of the letter, above and to the right of the address. The stamp or stamps should be stuck on the right way round, with the top edge aligned to the top edge of the envelope.

Writing letters to or within the UK

Postcodes in the UK consist of a combination of numbers and letters that are presented in two groups, eg EH1 9QX. The postcode is usually on a separate line, after the city or county. The town and postcode should be written in capitals.

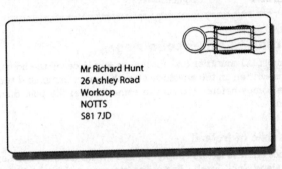

Mr Richard Hunt
26 Ashley Road
Worksop
NOTTS
S81 7JD

When sending letters to the United Kingdom, it is not necessary to specify the country: England, Scotland, Wales or Northern Ireland. Letters from abroad should end with the post town, the postcode, and United Kingdom or its foreign equivalent.

County names are now deemed unnecessary in the UK, provided that the post town and postcode are included. However, some people still prefer to use them. Here are abbreviations for some English counties:

County	Abbrev.	County	Abbrev.
Bedfordshire	Beds	Hampshire	Hants
Berkshire	Berks	Herefordshire	Hereford
Buckinghamshire	Bucks	Hertfordshire	Herts
Cambridgeshire	Cambs	Lancashire	Lancs
Derbyshire	Derbys	Leicestershire	Leics
Gloucestershire	Gloucs	Lincolnshire	Lincs

Northamptonshire	Northants	Staffordshire	Staffs
Nottinghamshire	Notts	Warwickshire	Warks
Oxfordshire	Oxon	Wiltshire	Wilts
Shropshire	Salop	Worcestershire	Wo
Somerset	Somt		

Writing to other countries

For most EU countries (except France and Greece), the house number is written on the envelope after the street name, and the postcode comes before (and on the same line as) the post district or town.

Republic of Ireland

Do not address letters simply 'Ireland': write instead 'The Republic of Ireland' (not 'Eire'). Postcodes are not used in the Republic of Ireland except in Dublin, where the numbers 1-24 designate various sectors of the city. In all other areas, the abbreviation **Co.** is used to indicate the county, eg **Co. Kerry** signifies the county of Kerry.

USA

The following guidelines are those issued by the US postal authorities to ensure that addresses on envelopes can be processed by the postal service's automated equipment. The address should be entirely in capital letters and without punctuation. The ZIP Code (the US postcode) must be separated from the state abbreviation by two spaces.

First line:	ADDRESSEE'S NAME
Second line:	NUMBER, STREET, APARTMENT NUMBER or POST OFFICE BOX NUMBER
Third line:	CITY, STATE, ZIP CODE (POSTCODE)
Fourth line:	UNITED STATES OF AMERICA

Ms S. Gulliver
34 Hawthorn Ave
St Davids
SA65 7NZ
United Kingdom

Ms WENDY ROBINSON
11867 CRESTA VERDE DRIVE
ST LOUIS MO 63145
UNITED STATES OF AMERICA

Below is a list of the official postal abbreviations of US states, to be used when addressing envelopes bound for the United States.

Alabama	AL	Massachusetts	MA
Alaska	AK	Michigan	MI
Arizona	AZ	Minnesota	MN
Arkansas	AR	Mississippi	MS
California	CA	Missouri	MO
Colorado	CO	Montana	MT
Connecticut	CT	Nebraska	NE
Delaware	DE	Nevada	NV
Florida	FL	New Hampshire	NH
Georgia	GA	New Jersey	NJ
Hawaii	HI	New Mexico	NM
Idaho	ID	New York	NY
Illinois	IL	North Carolina	NC
Indiana	IN	North Dakota	ND
Iowa	IA	Ohio	OH
Kansas	KS	Oklahoma	OK
Kentucky	KY	Oregon	OR
Louisiana	LA	Pennsylvania	PA
Maine	ME	Rhode Island	RI
Maryland	MD	South Carolina	SC

South Dakota	SD	Virginia	VA
Tennessee	TN	Washington	WA
Texas	TX	West Virginia	WV
Utah	UT	Wisconsin	WI
Vermont	VT	Wyoming	WY

Canada

In Canada, it is usual to write the name of the town or municipality, followed by the abbreviation corresponding to the province in which it is located, followed by the postcode, all on the same line. The postcode must be two spaces to the right of the province, with one space between the first three and last three characters. For example:

MADAME CHANTAL LEMOINE
3567 RUE DRUMMOND
MONTRÉAL QC H3G 1M8

Bilingual addresses must be separated by a solid black line between the two addresses. The line must be at least 0.7 mm thick and should have a clear space of about 10mm on either side. For example:

NATIONAL BANK
PO BOX 9700 STN A
TORONTO SN M5W 1R6

BANQUE NATIONALE
CP 9700 SUCC A
TORONTO SN M5W 1R6

Below is a list of the official postal abbreviations of Canadian provinces and territories.

Alberta	AB	Manitoba	MB
British Columbia	BC	New Brunswick	NB

Newfoundland	NF		Prince Edward Island	PE
Nova Scotia	NS		Quebec	QC
Northwest Territories	NT		Saskatchewan	SK
Nunavut	NU		Yukon	YT
Ontario	ON			

Australia

The final line of the address must contain the place name (or post office of delivery), state or territory abbreviation and 4-digit post-code, all written in capitals, with spaces between the items and without punctuation or underlining. For example:

Mr James Thorpe
7 Eucalyptus Drive
CAMMERAY NSW 2069

Below is a list of the official postal abbreviations of Australian states and territories.

Australian Capital Territory	ACT		South Australia	SA
			Tasmania	TAS
New South Wales	NSW		Victoria	VIC
Northern Territory	NT		Western Australia	WA
Queensland	QLD			

Spain

In Spanish addresses you will often find no word for 'street', only the actual name of the street, unless it is called, for example, 'Avenida' or 'Paseo'. You will also see the abbreviation C/ for 'Calle'. The house number comes after the street name, and the postcode precedes the name of the town or city. After the house number you will often see another number followed by superscript ^{a} or ^{o}. This indicates which floor of a building the apartment is situated on. For example, the third floor in the following example:

Gran Vía 13 3º
28005 Madrid

If a third number is given, this refers to the door number:

Gran Vía 13 3º 1ª
28005 Madrid

France

You might often see 'bis' and 'ter' after the street number in a French address. For example:

3 bis RUE DES LILAS
11 ter AVENUE DE BERNAY

They indicate that there is more than one residence, whether in the form of a self-contained apartment or an annexe to the main house or premises, at the address in question. 'Bis' is used to indicate that there is a second residential (or business) unit, 'ter' a third, the equivalent of 3b or 11c in English.

The first two numbers of a French postcode correspond to the administrative code number of the relevant 'département'. All postcodes for Paris begin with 75. For example:

20 BOULEVARD ARAGO
75013 PARIS

In the example above, the first two numbers indicate the city of Paris while the last two figures indicate that the address is located in the thirteenth 'arrondissement' (district) of the city.

> *Usage*
>
> The French postal services recommend that no punctuation be used on the envelope and that the name of the town should be written in capital letters, without any accents or hyphens.

Belgium

In Belgium, addresses are often written with the house number after the street name, and the postcode before the town. For an apartment or a house where there are more than three letterboxes it is usual to add the letterbox number (not the apartment number) after the street number. For example:

Monsieur Luc Dujardin
rue du Clocher 143, bte 12
1040 Bruxelles

> *i*
>
> **bte** is the abbreviation for *boîte* (box).

Switzerland

Swiss addresses are also usually written with the house number appearing after the street name, and the postcode before the town. If writing from outside Switzerland one may include the abbreviation CH (for 'Confederatio Helvetica' or the Swiss Confederation). For example:

Monsieur André Roux
Avenue du Peyrou 4
CH - 2000 Neuchâtel

ADDRESSES AND SENDING LETTERS TO OTHER COUNTRIES

Useful sources

The websites of the postal services of a country are a useful source of information regarding addresses and postcodes/zip codes in particular. Here are some addresses:

UK: www.royalmail.com
Canada: www.canadapost.ca
Ireland: www.anpost.ie
USA: www.usps.gov
Australia: www.auspost.com.au
New Zealand: www.nzpost.co.nz
Spain: www.correos.es
France: www.laposte.fr
Germany: www.deutschepost.de
Belgium: www.post.be
Luxembourg: www.ept.lu
Switzerland: www.poste.ch

Universal Postal Union: http://www.upu.int

Abbreviations used in addresses

In addresses, there are several conventional abbreviations used in customary titles (eg *Dr*, *Prof*, *The Rev*, *The Rt Hon*) and in the street names (eg *St*, *Ave*, *Blvd*, *Rd*). There should be no full stops in these abbreviations when written on the envelope.

The following abbreviations are commonly used in addresses:

Apt	Apartment	**Ct**	Court	**La**	Lane
Av or		**Dr**	Drive	**Mtn**	Mountain
Ave	Avenue	**Est**	Estate	**Pde**	Parade
Blvd	Boulevard	**Gdns**	Gardens	**Pk**	Park
Cl	Close	**Gr**	Grove	**Pl**	Place
Cres	Crescent	**Hts**	Heights	**Plz**	Plaza

Rdg	Ridge	**Rm**	Room	**St**	Street
Rd	Road	**Sq**	Square	**Ter**	Terrace

The abbreviations **N** (North), **S** (South), **W** (West), **E** (East), **NE** (Northeast), **NW** (Northwest), **SE** (Southeast) and **SW** (Southwest) are also common, especially in addresses in Canada and the United States:

351 W 32ND ST
NEW YORK, NY 100001

> This address reads as: **three hundred and fifty-one West Thirty-second Street**

123 MAIN ST NW
MONTREAL QC H3Z 2Y7

> This address reads as: **one hundred and twenty-three Main Street Northwest**

Part Two

Types of Letter

Business correspondence

This chapter looks at business correspondence: letters, memos and faxes.

Business letters

Business letters are generally formal in tone and should be brief, to the point, accurate and polite. They are always typed and are nowadays usually in blocked style (see pages 11–12) with the minimum of punctuation.

A letter or order should be acknowledged within two or three days of the date it was received, so that the sender knows that the matter is being dealt with. An acknowledgement may be in the form of a short letter or a postcard. It should state when the letter/order was received and confirm that the issue is being handled.

The layout of business letters

Business letters usually contain the following:

- The name, address and contact details of the business or organization sending the letter. Business letters are usually written on office stationery which contains the contact details in the letterhead.
- An internal reference, which often includes the initials of the person who has signed it. The firm's internal reference (usually beginning with *Our reference:* or *Our ref:*) should always be quoted in any reply to the letter, using the formula *Your reference:* or *Your ref:*.
- The name and address of the recipient.
- The date.

- A greeting or salutation (see pages 17–20).
- A heading that will help the recipient to see at a glance what your letter is about. The heading usually follows the opening greeting.
- The main body of the letter.
- The ending or complimentary close (see pages 18–20).

Organizing and structuring the content of a business letter

Like most documents, a business letter consists of three parts: an introduction, a development, and a conclusion:

- The **introduction** is a single paragraph, perhaps even a single sentence. It states the subject or purpose of your letter, and acknowledges any previous letter that was sent by the person you are writing to.
- The **development** has one or more paragraphs. This deals with the subject of your letter in as much detail as is necessary. You can use bullet points, numbered headings or subject headings to make the information clear to read and easy to understand.
- The **conclusion** is a single paragraph, usually containing some expression of goodwill. For business letters, it is better to say something fairly formal, for example *I look forward to meeting you* rather than *Looking forward to meeting you*.

Useful phrases:

General:

- I refer to your letter of 12 July 2005.
- Thank you for your letter dated 5 May.
- Further to our telephone conversation yesterday/this morning ...
- As we agreed/discussed on Friday ...
- There are several points that I would like to discuss further. Firstly, ... Secondly, ...

- I would like to arrange another meeting with you to discuss matters/the proposal further and will phone you early next week.
- We would appreciate having an opportunity to speak with you or one of your representatives about ...

Placing orders:

- We would like to place an order for the following items, in the sizes and quantities specified below.
- Please find enclosed our order no. 471 for ...
- I wish to order ... as advertised in the July issue of your catalogue.
- I would appreciate confirmation of the dates/of delivery.
- Could you please confirm the dates as soon as possible.

Responding to requests:

- Thank you for your enquiry of 13 March about our equipment/services/products ...
- In response to your enquiry of 7 March, we have pleasure in enclosing full details of ..., together with our price list.
- We regret that we will be unable to fulfil your order for ...
- We regret that the goods you ordered are temporarily out of stock/we no longer stock the goods you ordered.

Payment:

- Please find enclosed a cheque for ... in payment of your invoice no. B5666 of 10 October.
- We enclose a cheque for ... in payment of your invoice no. B5666.
- We apologize most sincerely for the non-payment/delayed payment of invoice no. B5666.
- Our records indicate that payment on your account is overdue to the amount of ...

- If the amount has already been paid, please disregard this notice.
- On 12 July we notified you of your overdue account for order no. 471.
- Please give this matter your most urgent attention.

Final paragraph:

- Thank you for your hospitality/arranging the meeting/your interest in our company.
- Once again, thank you for your interest in our products.
- Should you require any further information, please contact me.
- I look forward to hearing from you soon.
- I look forward to doing business with you.

LAYOUT OF A BUSINESS/OFFICIAL LETTER
(blocked style)

The Carpet Bazaar

5-7 Murray Road
NORWICH NO2 2RN
Tel: 01793 58607 Fax: 01793 44607
E-mail: carpetbazaar@flying.com
Website: www.carpetbazaar.com

Our ref: CAR/402
Date: 11 July 2005

F A Wikeley
54 Albany Road
GLOUCESTER
GL9 7RN

Dear Mr Wikeley

Carpet and kilim catalogue

Thank you for your enquiry of 2 July about our products. I enclose
our current catalogue and price list as requested.

We are constantly adding to our collection of carpets and kilims.
If you have access to the Internet, you could visit our website, which
is regularly updated to include our latest acquisitions.

If you require any further information, please do not hesitate to
contact us.

We look forward to hearing from you soon.

Thank you for your interest in our products.

Yours sincerely

Rosanna Lee

Rosanna Lee
Managing Director

Encs

LETTER/CARD OF ACKNOWLEDGEMENT FOR ORDER

Auto Direct
6 Netherdale Road
Glasgow G64 2JP
Tel: 0141 633 3255
Fax: 0141 633 3266

Our ref: T13607-99RT
Your ref: P126/GW

23/7/2005

Mr G Wendell
New Park Motor Supplies Ltd
300 Depot Road
Ayr
KA8 9PP

Dear Customer

This is to acknowledge receipt of your order no. 5698 dated 20 July 2005.

The order is receiving our immediate attention and will be dispatched to you by 30 July 2005.

I hope we may continue to receive your valued custom.

Paul Ryder

Paul Ryder
Sales Advisor

LETTER PLACING AN ORDER

Watts Office Supplies

88 Prince Edward Road
BRISTOL
BS9 0ZZ
Tel: 0117 564 8956
www.wattsoffice.co.uk

Customer Service Manager
Middlemarch Diaries
6 Consort Way
TUNBRIDGE WELLS
Kent
TN1 6BG

5 October 2006

Dear Sir/Madam

2007 Diary Order

I refer to your letter of 30 September enclosing your catalogue of diaries for 2007. I would like to place an order for some of the products advertised.

I enclose a completed order form. I assume that the amount payable will be subject to the usual trade discount. Please advise if this is not the case. Please also advise of the preferred method of payment.

I look forward to receiving your confirmation of my order, and would be obliged if you would advise me in advance of the planned delivery date, so that I can reorganize my stock accordingly.

Since I want to display next year's diaries from early November, I would be grateful if you would give this matter your urgent attention.

Yours faithfully

James Watts

J Watts
Chief Buyer

cc B Jones

LETTER TO ARRANGE A MEETING

LOOK NOW
73 Cumberland Road
Belfast
BT7 8UR
Tel: 028 9045333
Email: looknow@norcom.co.uk

Our Ref: S901R3
Your Ref: s/02P

Mr Patrick Meers
Distribution Manager
Meers Ltd
16 Roehampton Road
London
SW15 5LU

20 September 2006

Dear Mr Meers

Thank you for your letter dated 12 September. I was extremely interested to read your proposals and would like to arrange a meeting with you to discuss them further.

I would be available to come to London during the last week of November, if that is convenient for you. I would be accompanied by my personal assistant, Martine Barry, and can arrange to bring samples of both our spring and summer lines.

I would be grateful if you could confirm the dates as soon as possible. If you require any further details, please do not hesitate to contact me.

I look forward to meeting you.

Yours sincerely

Suzanne McLoughlin

Suzanne McLoughlin
Managing Director

LETTER FROM SUPPLIER REQUESTING REFERENCE

Maygold plc
456-460 Queens Road
CARDIFF
CF22 0ZZ
Tel: 02920 6654892

Our ref: NAS/10/MM
Your ref: D889/HW

Mr R Fleck
NorthEast Paper Products Ltd
78 Ship Road
NEWCASTLE
NE9 0ZZ

25 July 2005

Dear Mr Fleck

Thank you for your order of 20 July 2005, which is receiving our prompt attention.

As you are a new customer, we would be grateful if you would supply us with a standard banker's reference for our records. Alternatively we would be pleased to receive your remittance before your order is dispatched.

Yours sincerely

Marjorie Mead

Marjorie Mead
Accounts

LETTER REPLYING TO INVOICE

Watts Office Supplies

88 Prince Edward Road
BRISTOL
BS9 0ZZ
Tel: 0117 564 8956
www.wattsoffice.co.uk

Our ref: KEL/10/MM
Your ref: WATT/767

D George
KELPACK Ltd
44-48 Westhill Street
BIRMINGHAM
BB5 0JJ

15 October 2005

Dear Mr George

Payment of Invoice no. BD767

Thank you for the prompt delivery of our order no. C00145.

Please find enclosed a cheque for £327.50 in payment of your invoice no. BD767 of 30 September 2005.

We look forward to doing further business with you in the near future.

Yours sincerely

David Wallace

D Wallace
Buying assistant

SALES PROMOTION LETTER

MADDOCK PUBLISHING Ltd
Hillview Industrial Estate
LONDON
Tel: 0207 345 6655
Email: sales@maddock.co.uk

Simon Software
2 Landmark Square
Manchester
M28 2SG

30 July 2005

Dear Sir or Madam

Publishing Opportunities in Europe

We are an established publisher of European trade and business
journals with high visibility throughout the European Union and
Eastern Europe. Currently we are offering special advertising rates
and benefits to new customers.

This is an excellent opportunity for your company to increase its
share of the IT market in the dynamic European market place.

Please find enclosed two copies of our journals, with our
compliments. If you wish to pursue our offer or require any further
information, please contact our enquiry line on Freefone 08457 37 65.

I look forward to hearing from you.

Yours faithfully

J. C. Mitchison

J. C. Mitchison
Sales Director

Memos

Memos (or memorandums) are used for sending messages to employees or colleagues within a business or organization, though not necessarily in the same building. In modern practice, the paper memo has largely been replaced by **e-mail** (see Part 3).

Usage

Remember that a memo is an official business communication – however informal, and on whatever subject – and that a copy might therefore need to be kept on record.

A memo generally has a number of items of information printed at the top, for example:

- name(s) of the recipient, including a department or job title; the recipient may be a group of people, such as a committee or a department
- name of the sender, often including a telephone number or extension and department
- names of anyone else who is to get a copy of this memo (the letters *cc*, standing for 'carbon copy' are used to indicate this)
- reference number (if the organization records memos using serial numbers or a similar cataloguing system)
- date
- subject (the word *re*, which is Latin for 'on the subject of' is used to indicate this)

Although a memo is a type of letter, it does not have a salutation (*Dear Mhairi*), or a complimentary close (*Yours sincerely*). As with business letters, if an enclosure is sent with a memo, the word *enc* or *encs* should be added at the end, usually aligned with the text against the left-hand margin.

Keep the following points in mind:
Length: Memos should be concise, with an absolute maximum length of two pages.

Objective: Memos usually have a specific aim – keep yours in mind. If action is required, outline what it is and when it is required.

Organization: Begin with the main information, progress to any supporting facts and finish with any request or call for action. Use headings to emphasize key topics. Bold typeface or underlining can highlight important figures, dates, etc.

Style: Use clear, jargon-free language.

Tone: The recent trend has been towards a more conversational tone. Avoid passive sentence structures and use pronouns such as 'I', 'we' and 'you' instead.

MEMO

To: **Personnel**
From: **Nicky James, Human Resources, Ext 211**
Cc:
Date: **24 May 2005**
Re: **Meeting to discuss the update of the in-house magazine**

In order to discuss proposals for an updated in-house magazine we are holding a meeting in **Room 189**, 2nd Floor on **Friday, 29 May** at **11am**.

Agenda:
 1. Suggested amendments to the magazine.
 2. Decision on a suitable time frame for completion of update.
 3. Formation of sub-committee to liaise with the Design Department.

Request for Suggestions:
I would welcome any suggestions you have regarding the update relating to design, format or subject-matter. I can be contacted at the above extension.

Attendance:
Please let me know if you are unable to attend.

Fax (facsimile)

Fax is another quick and convenient way of sending documents (both handwritten and printed), using telephone lines.

Fax is widely used in business and is useful for sending messages and documents that must reach their destination quickly, but for one reason or another cannot be sent via the Internet. However, scanners linked to computers can convert documents into computer files which may then be sent via the Internet, and it is likely that fax machines will decrease in popularity as computer technology advances and becomes more affordable. Many personal computers now include a facility for fax, and this has an added advantage in that you can read the fax and store it on your computer hard disk, without ever having to print it out.

Here are some general points:

- A faxed document should always be accompanied by a cover sheet, which should include details of the sender, how many pages are being sent, who the message is intended for and whether or not it is confidential.
- It is not always necessary to include a greeting line, particularly if you know the person. When faxing someone whom you do not know well, you can use an opening greeting. If you do not know their name, use the standard opening *Dear Sir or Madam*.
- Similarly, a complimentary close is not always included. However, for the sake of politeness and to achieve a friendlier tone, you could close with a phrase such as *Best wishes* or *Regards*.
- The language of fax messages tends to be more informal and the style is often telegraphic. Abbreviations are commonly used, particularly for days and months.

FAX

35 Willowdale
Newcastle NE2 4SS
Phone: 0551 667696
Fax: 0771 225252

Sunwell Printing

Fax

To:	Tom Frost	From:	Julian Brennan
Fax:	0551 668 9599	Date:	March 8 2005
Phone:	0551 668 9598	Pages:	1
Re:	Itinerary for visit to Cardiff	CC:	

❏ **Urgent** ❏ **For Review** ❏ **Please Comment**

❏ **Please Reply** ❏ **Please Recycle**

Comments:

Arrival date now Tues 12 March. Arr. Cardiff airport,
18.40. Please arrange visit to Matthews Paperworks
Wed am and meeting at your office Wed pm. Flight
Cardiff-Newcastle Thurs 09.00.

Call Sally asap to confirm.

Thanks and regards

Julian Brennan

Some abbreviations and acronyms used in business correspondence

a/c	account	dept.	department
add.	addendum	Dir.	Director
AGM	annual general meeting	ea.	each
APR	annual percentage rate	E&OE	errors and omissions excepted
approx.	approximately		
asap	as soon as possible	eg, e.g.	for example (Latin *exempli gratia*)
attn.	attention		
av.	average	encl.	enclosed
bal.	balance	enc(s)	enclosure(s)
b/d	banker's draft (banking)	et al	and other (people or things) (Latin *et alii*, *aliae* or *alia*)
bc.	blind copy (of a memo, letter)		
bcc.	blind carbon copy	etc	and so on (Latin *et cetera*)
B/E, b/e	bill of exchange		
B/L, b/l	bill of lading	FAO, fao	for the attention of
c., ca	circa (approximately)	ff	following pages
C&F	cost and freight	fwd	forward
cc	carbon copy (copies to)	ie, i.e.	in other words (Latin *id est*)
CEO	Chief Executive Officer		
CFO	Chief Financial Officer	Inc.,	
chq	cheque	Incorp.	incorporated
C/N	consignment note; cover note; credit note	inc., incl.	included, including, inclusive
c/o	care of; carried over; cash order	infm.,	
		info	information
Co	company, county	inst	of this month
COD	cash on delivery	L/C	letter of credit
contd,		Ltd	limited company
cont'd	continued	MD	managing director
CV	curriculum vitae	mgr	manager
DD	direct debit	misc.	miscellaneous
del.	delivery; delivered	mtg	meeting

N/A	not applicable	**PTO**	please turn over
NB	note well (Latin *nota bene*)	**qty**	quantity
		re	regarding, about
NIS	not in stock	**rec.**	recommend
O/D	overdraft	**recd**	received
ono	or nearest offer	**Ref**	reference
OOS	out of stock	**req(d)**	required
p.a.	per annum (each year)	**retd**	retired
p&p	postage and packing	**sae**	stamped addressed envelope
PAYE	pay as you earn		
P/L	profit and loss	**sase**	self-addressed stamped envelope
plc, Plc,			
PLC	public limited company	**SO**	standing order
p.o.	postal order	**SOR**	sale or return
pp	on behalf of (Latin *per procurationem*)	**tba**	to be announced
		tbc	to be confirmed
pps	additional postscript	**ult.**	last
Pres.	president	**viz**	namely
ps	postscript	**VP**	Vice-President

Complaints and replies

Letters of complaint

i

Never write a letter while you are angry. (Chinese Proverb)

Avoid writing a letter of complaint in a white heat of rage or indignation. While it may relieve your feelings, the result is likely to be rather incoherent and, in the long run, probably less effective than a letter that is polite but firm and sticks to the facts. This applies equally when you are writing to complain about something that has offended you and when you are complaining about goods and services.

Complaints about goods and services

When you are complaining about goods or services, remember that the person who reads the letter may not personally be responsible for the problem. Be firm but understanding. The following points should be helpful:

- Make sure that you have all the relevant facts so you can quote prices, names, times, addresses and dates. This shows the reader that you are in control of the situation, and also helps your complaint to be dealt with more efficiently. If necessary, be prepared to quote any relevant pieces of consumer law.
- Make sure to include your contact details.
- If there is no named individual to whom you can address your complaint, direct your letter to the Customer Services Manager or, for smaller companies and family businesses, the owner or managing director (he or she is the person who will be most

concerned about the firm's image and therefore most likely to take prompt action).

- Give your letter a heading. This should include any product details such as the order number, product number or model, together with the reference number of your receipt or invoice if you have it.
- Give details of the problem, stating that you are dissatisfied, and saying why.
- Send copies of any relevant documents, such as warranties or receipts – keep the originals.
- State clearly what you would like to be done about the problem, if necessary giving a date by which you would like matters to be resolved. Do you want a refund? Do you want to exchange the product? Do you just want an apology?
- Make sure you make a claim for a refund or compensation within any time limit defined under the relevant Act.
- Refer to any further action you intend to take if your letter does not receive a satisfactory reply. If you feel you must pursue legal action, tell the reader in a direct, respectful way.
- If you do not receive, at the very least, an acknowledgement within the time limit you have set, write again.
- Keep copies of all the letters you send and make a note of all the telephone calls you make, including times, dates, how long they lasted, and who you spoke to. If you are making a claim of any kind, you may need documentary evidence if the claim is contested.
- It is a good idea to send your letter by recorded delivery. A signature is required for the letter when it is delivered, and the other party will not therefore be able to claim they have not received it.

Useful phrases:

- I wish to draw your attention to …
- I wish to complain about …
- I wish to express my dissatisfaction regarding …

COMPLAINTS AND REPLIES

- I am extremely concerned that ...
- When the goods arrived I found the following defects/ damage ...
- I experienced the following problems ...
- The service we were offered was unsatisfactory in the following ways ...
- Under the terms of your guarantee ...
- It was implied in the contract between us ...
- I look forward to receiving your written reply within the next seven days.
- I look forward to your suggestions as to how the situation can be put right ...
- I would be interested in any comments you might wish to make ...
- If we are still not satisfied ...

LETTER COMPLAINING ABOUT FAULTY GOODS

7 Morningside Drive
EDINBURGH
EH9 4AY

The Customer Services Manager
Whitegoods plc
Lowburn Industrial Park
EDINBURGH EH39 1GG

4th August 2005

Dear Sir or Madam

Kleanquik Automatic Washing Machine. Model number 9337.

I purchased the above model of washing machine from your Wallace Street store on 15th July 2005. It was delivered and installed by your service engineer on 19th July 2005.

On 30th July 2005, only eleven days after the machine was installed, it developed a serious fault, causing water to flood out of the front of the machine. I immediately telephoned the store and they advised me that an engineer would call on Tuesday 2nd August at 11 a.m. I waited at home but no engineer called. I have telephoned the store repeatedly and each time was informed that someone would call me back. No one did.

I must therefore insist that you inform me in writing of your proposals to remedy this situation by providing me with a firm date and time when your engineer will call. While I am prepared to give you a further opportunity to honour your guarantee, I reserve my right to claim compensation for the inconvenience already caused to me and to reject the goods as unsatisfactory under the terms of the Sale of Goods Act 1979.

Yours faithfully

Jane Pearson

Jane Pearson (Mrs)

LETTER COMPLAINING ABOUT DEFECTIVE WORKMANSHIP

6 Eastrow Cottages
Newport
NP3 4DD

John Carpenter & Sons
38 Cardiff Road
Newport
NP1 9FF

21 September 2005

Dear Sirs

Defective lock

I wish to complain about one of the new locks your firm fitted on my front door on 19th August 2005, after my home had been broken into the previous evening. I paid you £197.50 inclusive of VAT for the work. I enclose a copy of your receipted invoice for that amount.

The defective lock has two loose screws on the interior side of the door, which were obviously not anchored sufficiently firmly to the wood. As a result the lock is no longer properly aligned with the door jamb, making it difficult to turn the key.

Please confirm that you will rectify the defect as a matter of urgency, at no additional cost to me. I must emphasize that time is of the essence. If the necessary work is not carried out within the next 7 days, I shall have no alternative but to employ another firm, and am legally entitled to recover the costs incurred from you.

Yours faithfully

A.S. Swinton

A.S. Swinton (Mrs)

LETTER COMPLAINING ABOUT UNSATISFACTORY SERVICE

20 Selsdon Way
YORK
YO7 7DS

The Customer Services Manager
East Coast Mainline
King's Cross Station
LONDON
N1 3ZZ

23 March 2005

Dear Sir or Madam

Delayed York-London train

I am writing to complain about the inconvenience caused to me last week by your company's inadequate performance.

I was booked to travel on the 08:00 train from York to London on 19 March. This was due to arrive in London at 11:00. I had been assured, when I booked my ticket, that this would give me plenty of time to change platforms and catch the 11:35 train to Bedford, where I had an important appointment. However, we arrived in London at 11:47, more than three-quarters of an hour late. I therefore missed my connection.

I am more than disappointed with the service I received and feel I am entitled to compensation which reflects adequately the inconvenience suffered.

I look forward to receiving your response within the next 14 days.

Yours faithfully

B. Anderson

B. Anderson

Responding to a complaint

Large commercial organizations receive many letters every year from people who have put pen to paper – often on the spur of the moment – to complain. Letters dealing with complaints are not simple exchanges of information, but require tact and delicacy:

- No matter how abusive the writer may be, no matter how wild their views are, a courteous and measured response is the only appropriate one. Even if you do not agree with the complaint, and can do nothing about it, a considerate response will often help soothe an irate client.

- Commercial organizations should always respond to customer complaints about goods and services, and in the shortest possible time. Any delay seems rude and can make the situation worse. The sooner you respond to a client, the greater the chances of resolving the problem as quickly as possible.

- If the letter lists a number of complaints or raises a number of points, make sure that you deal with all of them, in a bulleted list if necessary.

- When you don't have enough information to respond to the complaint immediately, either ask the customer for more information or inform the customer that you are collecting more information from another source before responding. It lets the customer know that you take the complaint seriously.

- Apologize for any errors or delays.

- If you are at fault and are able to make amends, apologize for the inconvenience and outline clearly how you wish to remedy the problem. Offer some gesture of goodwill if possible.

- If the customer has complained, but is not seeking any action (such as a refund etc), it is often worthwhile to respond to a complaint by treating it as valuable feedback. This is a good public relations exercise. It lets the customer feel appreciated and it gives you an opportunity to explain what you are doing to make things better.

- If you cannot fulfil the complainant's request for redress, explain politely why you cannot do so. The denial will probably disappoint the customer, so be tactful.

Useful phrases:

- I was concerned to learn that ...
- I would like to apologize for any inconvenience this has caused.
- I appreciate that this must be frustrating ...
- ... put things right at the earliest available opportunity.
- Thank you for your patience.
- If you have any questions, please contact ...
- I am pleased to be able to inform you that ...
- To compensate for the inconvenience caused to you/your company, we would like to ...
- Please find enclosed ... with our compliments.

LETTER RESPONDING TO A COMPLAINT

John Carpenter & Sons
38 Cardiff Road
Newport
NP1 9FF
Tel: 01633 567 228

Mrs A S Swinton
6 Eastrow Cottages
Newport
NP3 4DD

23 September 2005

Dear Mrs Swinton

Defective lock

Thank you for your letter of 21 September in which you advised that one of the new locks, which were fitted at your property recently by one of our joiners, is not working satisfactorily.

I am very concerned that if there is any question of faulty workmanship or a defect with the lock itself this should be put right at the earliest opportunity. Therefore, I suggest that I call round on Friday morning at 9 am so that I can examine the lock personally and have any necessary repairs carried out immediately. You may be assured that if the fault lies with us that any repair or replacement will be carried out at no additional cost to you.

Please telephone me directly if the suggested arrangement is not to your convenience.

Yours sincerely

Robert Carpenter

Robert Carpenter
Director

LETTER RESPONDING TO A COMPLAINT ABOUT LATE DELIVERY OF GOODS

WOODS OF COVENTRY

21 Regina Drive
Coventry
CV9 2EQ
Tel: 02476 621699
E-mail: woods@busynet.co.uk

Our ref: NAS/324
Your ref: WOOD/HW

Mr Jackson Bratte
13 Pennybrook Lane
Dollis Hill
London
NW2 6HG

7 September 2005

Dear Mr Bratte

Order 324 B

Thank you for your letter of 3 September, bringing to our attention the delay in the delivery of your computers for the above order. I should like to apologize for the delay and the inconvenience this has caused you.

We have experienced supply problems from our factory that have now been remedied. The computers are expected to arrive at our depot later this week and I shall contact you on their arrival to arrange a speedy delivery.

Thank you for your patience and I look forward to advising you later this week.

Yours sincerely

Theo Smith

Theo Smith
Customer Services Manager

Employment

This chapter gives guidance on writing letters to prospective employers, on how to present your CV (or, in American English, 'résumé'), on accepting and declining offers of employment and on letters of resignation.

Job applications

A letter in which you apply for a job should be written with care. First impressions count, and your letter and CV are the only things that a potential employer has on which to base his or her impression of you.

Use identical stationery for the covering letter and CV. Use good quality, heavy paper, preferably white or cream, and black ink. If you are writing by hand use a good pen, or if writing on-screen, use a typeface that is clear and legible (such as Arial or Times New Roman) and a type size not less than 11 point.

Most importantly, make sure your letter and CV are free of grammatical errors, misspellings and mistakes. Ensure names and dates are correct. If writing a letter by hand, make a rough draft first. If you make a mistake in the final version, start again. Correction fluid and deletions look messy and unprofessional. Ask someone else to read your letter and CV to check for any mistakes.

Covering letter

The covering letter is the letter that accompanies the CV or application. The person who reads your letter will probably have read hundreds of other letters over the months or years, so it is worth taking a bit of time to try to get things right. The letter should be clear, concise and to the point. Here are some useful points to remember when writing the covering letter:

- The covering letter should be handwritten if this is specified in the advertisement. Otherwise it may be typed and signed by hand.
- Remember to include your home address, telephone number, e-mail address, and the date.
- Take care to get the name and title of the person or organization you are writing to exactly right. Avoid writing to *The Personnel Manager*. Call the company or check their website to find out the name and position of the relevant person.
- Tailor your letter to each specific job. Employers will be able to recognize a generic formulaic letter which you send unchanged with every application. You need to demonstrate that you have thought about why you are applying for that specific position and why you think you are particularly suited to it.
- Keep in mind that the aim of the covering letter is to give only enough information to engender interest and to encourage your reader to offer you an interview. Your CV/résumé will include all your personal details and work history, it is not necessary to duplicate all this information in the letter which accompanies it.
- Begin the letter with a short paragraph which gives a clear and prominent indication of which job you are applying for – use a reference number if provided. Say where you saw the post advertised and mention that you are enclosing your CV/résumé.
- The first paragraph should be followed by a fuller paragraph highlighting any qualifications, skills or experience that you consider are particularly relevant, or giving any other reason why you believe you are a suitable candidate for the post. Include brief examples to back up any claims. Pay attention to the advertisement – are you answering their requirements?
- Demonstrate your knowledge of the company. This will show that you have done your research, that you are organized and

thorough and that you have made an informed decision about applying for the position.

- Conclude with a short paragraph offering availability for interview.

Useful phrases:

- I would like to apply for the position of ... as advertised.
- I am writing in response to your advertisement in ... for ...
- I would like to be considered for the above post which your company advertised in ...
- I enclose my CV for your consideration.
- I believe I am a suitable candidate because ...
- I am confident that I can perform the job effectively because ...
- I am computer literate/a good communicator/a good organizer.
- I have good computer/IT/written and verbal communication skills.
- I have a good knowledge/thorough understanding of general office software packages/purchasing systems.
- I enjoy a challenge and relish learning new tasks.
- I work well in a team/under pressure.
- I perform well under time constraints.
- I can handle multiple tasks simultaneously.
- My experiences in ... have taught me how to ...
- I believe that my experience/qualification/skills would be of benefit to your company.
- Thank you for considering my application.
- I look forward to discussing this application in more detail with you.

COVERING LETTER FOR AN ADVERTISED POSITION (experienced candidate)

40 Crescent Lane
Brighton
BN2 1BN

Tel: 01273 556998
Mobile: 045875 555662
E-mail: mbenson@eazynet.com

Mr D Smithwick
Chief Analyst
Dunworkin Investments
Threadneedle Street
London
E3 6PG

19 May 2006

Dear Mr Smithwick

Financial Analyst

I would like to apply for the above position as advertised in *The Guardian* of 14 May, and I enclose my CV for your attention.

I am an experienced financial analyst and consultant, having worked extensively in this sector in Frankfurt and more recently in London. I am currently looking for a position that will allow me to develop my skills and experience in a small, dynamic commercial team such as Dunworkin Investments.

I believe that my academic qualifications and international financial experience would be of benefit to your company. I also have a thorough understanding of the relevant software systems as well as excellent verbal and written communication skills.

I thank you for your consideration and remain at your disposal for any further information. I look forward to meeting you in the near future.

Yours sincerely

Mark Benson

Mark Benson
Financial Investment Analyst

Enc.

COVERING LETTER FOR AN ADVERTISED POSITION

Flat 1
64 Plockenden Road
Islington
LONDON
N1 0ZZ

Tel: 01234 567 8910

Alexander Maxwell
Personnel Manager
Kingsway Shopping Centre
Walford
LONDON
N2 0ZZ

12th October 2005

Dear Mr Maxwell

Shopping Centre Supervisor

I am writing in response to your advertisement in this week's 'Retail News' for a shopping centre supervisor.

I am twenty years old, and have just completed a year's training in business studies at Thames College. I left school last summer with 5 GCSEs and 2 A Levels (English and Maths). During holidays and at weekends, I have worked in a clothes shop as a sales assistant, and also in a newsagent's, where I was often left in charge. I am keen to follow a career in the retail industry, and think this post will give me the responsibility I am looking for.

Should you consider me suitable for the post, I can provide the names of three referees.

I look forward to hearing from you, and should you wish to, please do not hesitate to contact me at home at the above number.

Yours sincerely

Jonathan Lee

Jonathan Lee

Unsolicited application (with CV/résumé)

If you are writing a speculative letter to a company, your covering letter should include the following details:

- your home address, e-mail address and telephone number
- where you heard about the company; if you have heard about a possible vacancy from a contact, name them; demonstrate a knowledge of the company and why you would like to work for them
- your present job (if you have one) and any previous employment
- any other experience, qualifications or interests relevant to the post
- your availability for interview

UNSOLICITED APPLICATION

29 Bletchley Road
Worthing
West Sussex
BN14 7QY

Tel: 01903 990092

Alexander Maxwell
Personnel Manager
Kingsway Ltd
24-28 Finchley Rd
London
N2 0TT

13 December 2005

Dear Mr Maxwell

I wish to enquire about any vacancy you may have in your Sales Department.
Your customer services manager, Don Griffiths, suggested I wrote to you.

As you can see from the enclosed CV, I have a good educational background
and twelve years' experience in sales, both as sales representative and sales
executive.

I am currently working for a software company in Kent, where I have
acquired essential IT skills. I believe this combined experience in sales and
computing would be ideal for the job profile.

Should you consider my application favourably, I should be pleased to attend
an interview at any time.

Yours sincerely

William Brownston

William Brownston

Enclosure

Letter of application for a work placement

Many companies offer temporary work placements. When applying, enclose your CV with a covering letter. In the letter:

- include all your contact details
- detail your studies or any professional qualifications, and why they are relevant
- mention why you would like to work for the company to which you are applying, demonstrating that you have done your research and have made an informed decision in applying to them
- include any relevant previous experience, such as other work placements or summer jobs
- highlight your skills and your career objectives

---

i

In American English, the word **internship** is used instead of **work placement**.

LETTER OF APPLICATION FOR A WORK PLACEMENT

189 Belvedere Road
Manchester
M8 8SS
Tel: 0161 762 0854
E-mail: carmengrant@bravo.com

Ms Sarah Hamilton
Personnel Manager
Hill's Press
18 Douglas Avenue
Worsley
Manchester M28 2SG

20 March 2006

Dear Ms Hamilton

Work Placement

I am writing about the possibility of obtaining a work placement in the editorial department of your company.

I will be graduating from university in June with a Bachelor of Arts degree. My studies included courses in English and German language and literature, desktop publishing and applied linguistics.

I am a good communicator and a capable linguist. I enjoy working as part of a team and have good organizational skills. I am very interested in publishing and would appreciate an opportunity to work for a dynamic and internationally recognized firm such as Hill's Press.

I enclose my CV for your consideration. I would be available for an interview at your convenience.

Yours sincerely,

Carmen Grant

Carmen Grant

Enc.

CV (Curriculum Vitae)

A CV, which is a summary of your education and career to date, is one of the most important documents you will have to write. It is a marketing tool to secure you an interview. It is worth taking time to do thorough research, to plan your CV and construct it. Make sure it is well-presented, professional and customized to the relevant job so that it highlights your skills and experience. Remember to look at the CV from the employer's perspective. Are you giving prospective employers what they want? What makes your CV stand out from all the others?

Writing a CV

When planning or writing your CV, keep the following points in mind:

Appearance: it is vital that your CV is neat, professional, clear and easy to read. Use black ink on good white paper that matches your covering letter.

Length: ensure that your CV is not too long – about 2 pages is ideal. Omit any inessential personal details such as marital status, but ensure that your contact details are complete and correct.

Appropriate: it is often unnecessary to include hobbies unless they are relevant to the position or reveal some positive trait. It may be wise to avoid mention of membership of any political parties, pressure groups or religions, unless appropriate to the position. Is your e-mail address appropriate? Prospective employers may not wish to send an e-mail to 'hotlips@bluemoon.com'.

Format: steer clear of fancy intricate styles, fonts or layouts unless you are applying for a creative position such as a graphic designer or web-page creator, in which case your CV might be a way of demonstrating your design skills. In general, use a reader-friendly combination of brief paragraphs to outline job responsibilities and bullet points to highlight skills and achievements.

Targeted: customize your CV for each job. Highlight the skills and experience on your CV that correspond to those mentioned in the job advertisement.

Accomplishments: avoid long job descriptions – outline your main responsibilities and then emphasize your accomplishments and achievements. Have you won a contract, increased your turnover or successfully reduced waiting times? Have you implemented new rules or modernized systems or methods of working? Include figures to substantiate your claims.

Positive language: use active verbs to underline your accomplishments. Suitable words include: *implement, coordinate, manage, organize, train, produce, fulfil, perform, complete, establish.*

Accurate: grammar and spelling mistakes in CVs are the main source of irritation for employers and recruiters. Read yours thoroughly for misspellings and typing errors and ask a friend to check it for you. This may be your only chance to make a good first impression.

Types of CV

There are two types of CV: chronological and skills-based.

Chronological CV:

This is the most common type of CV and includes the following:

- **Contact Details**
- **Employment History/Professional Experience:** arrange these in reverse chronological order beginning with your current or most recent position.
- **Early Career:** you can include a brief summary of previous employment that may not be strictly relevant to the current position.
- **Educational Qualifications:** these should be included at the beginning or after the employment history.
- **Other headings:** these can include the following: Professional Qualifications/Membership; Computer Skills; Publications; Language Skills and Awards.

CHRONOLOGICAL CV

TOBY GRANT
198, Francis Avenue, Leicester LE4 9PQ
Tel: 01440 767 3393
E-mail: tgrant@myad.net
Date of Birth: 6 October 1965

WORK EXPERIENCE

1994 to present
Gannet UK Ltd, Greenwich, London - **Corporate Training Manager**
- Delegation and implementation of training throughout corporation
- Marketing and Sales of training materials to French and UK markets
- Delegate to European Training Council
- Design of new courses and presentation to new customers

1990-1994
Simon & Co plc, Leicester - **Training Consultant**
- Design and management of technical training programmes
- Running workshops, seminars and group projects
- Organization of international conferences

LANGUAGES

French: advanced oral and written skills
German: intermediate-level oral and written skills

COMPUTER SKILLS

Microsoft Word, Excel, PowerPoint, Access

EDUCATION

1986-1990
BA in Business Studies with French
Manchester University

1984-1986
HNC Business and Economics
Meadowbrook College, Leeds

CHRONOLOGICAL CV

JESSICA BRODIE
234 Sunset Drive
Edinburgh
EH16 5S8
Tel: 0131 456 7890
E-mail: jbrodie@ya.com

OBJECTIVE
Senior Consultant/Designer in telecoms or banking industry

EMPLOYMENT HISTORY
1997–present
IT Consultant and Systems Designer, Systems Go Ltd, Edinburgh
* Design and test new IT systems
* Head up team of consultants

Achievements:
* Oversaw the implementation of new testing procedures which have increased accuracy by 50% and reduced project turnaround times by 15%
* Successfully coordinated projects for external clients with budgets in excess of £250,000

1993–1997
Assistant Systems Consultant, Visionary PLC, Glasgow

Achievements:
* Implemented secure online order-tracking system for external client
* Designed and implemented a system for medium-size network (50-plus workstations)

June–August 1993
Work placement, JCN Design, Leeds
Worked as software design engineer

EDUCATION
1990–3
BSc in Computer Science (Hons)
University of Leeds

COMPUTER SKILLS
Languages and Software: C, C++, Java, XML
Operating Systems: Unix, Windows 2000 XP, Mac OS
Database administration (Oracle, SQL Server)

Skills-based or Functional CV:

This type of CV is useful for:

- those who are seeking a career-change and whose employment history may not be entirely appropriate for the job for which they are applying
- recent graduates who may not have a lengthy employment history
- those re-entering the job market who may not have an up-to-date employment record

This type of CV often begins with a personal profile or summary in which key traits, competencies and career objectives (long- or short-term) are highlighted. Skills and experience are then grouped together into categories that emphasize your suitability for the position.

This can be followed by a brief employment history – usually listing positions, company names and employment dates – and educational qualifications. Additional information, such as any publications or awards or relevant hobbies, can be included.

SKILLS-BASED OR FUNCTIONAL CV (recent graduate)

SONIA PETERSON

Email: speterson@easynet.co.uk

Date of Birth: 26.5.83

27 Beech Close
Skipton
North Yorkshire
BD26 5SR
Tel: 01709 456 789
Mobile: 08888 222257

PERSONAL PROFILE:

A conscientious individual seeking a career in international marketing, I possess excellent bilingual verbal and written communication skills. I am capable of achieving personal objectives as demonstrated by successful completion of my degree and my commitment to work-experience activities. I also have experience of working in Germany and the USA that provided exposure to alternative business cultures and protocols.

SKILLS AND ACHIEVEMENTS:

Communication

- Good communication skills gained from giving presentations at seminars and chairing meetings. Developed negotiation skills.
- Bilingual skills enhanced during work experience in Germany.
- Advising customers and handling problems and complaints during summer experience as a tourist advisor, which usually involved speaking in German.

Team Work

- Successful course work was dependent upon participation in and motivation of project groups.
- Experience of working within a team-based culture involved planning, organization, coordination and commitment.

Marketing Skills

Assisted with implementation of a new European e-marketing promotion strategy as part of work experience in the marketing department of an international company.

Completed dissertation on 'The importance of the Internet as a marketing tool', which involved extensive research.

Problem Analysis and Solving
· Development of strong analytic and diagnostic skills as part of degree course.
· Working as a tourist advisor to solve customer problems in a diplomatic and efficient manner.

Languages
Fluent written and spoken German developed through one year's work experience in Frankfurt.

Computing
Good working knowledge of several packages including: Microsoft Word, Access and Excel.

EDUCATION AND QUALIFICATIONS:

2001–2005 University of Ulster at Magee	BA (Hons) Business Studies with German (2.1 expected) (2003-2004 work experience in Germany)
1995–2000 Skipton Comprehensive	3 A-levels - English (B), Accounting (C), German (A). 7 GCSEs.

WORK EXPERIENCE:

July 2005–present Yorkshire Tourist Office, Skipton	Tourist Advisor
Sept 2003–June 2004 Marketing Department, MDW Investment Bank, Frankfurt	Marketing Assistant
July–Sept 2002 Camp America	Camp counsellor to 11–19 year-olds at summer camp

REFEREES:
Dr. Jim McKenna, Head of Business Studies, University of Ulster
Frau Anna Schmidt, Marketing Manager, MDW Investment Bank, Frankfurt

Applying for jobs online

It is now common to use the Internet to apply for jobs or to send your CV to recruiters and potential employers. There are several points to bear in mind:

- A concise covering letter in the form of an e-mail message is still required.
- Keep the formatting simple so that the CV will be easy to upload and open and will appear on-screen in the correct layout. It is usually best to attach it as a Word document.
- Use an appropriate file name for the attachment. Do not call it CV.doc – employers and recruiters will not be able to distinguish it from the hundreds of other CVs they receive. The most straightforward option is to use your name, as in: WilliamWallaceCV.doc

Accepting a job offer

Confirm your acceptance of a job offer in writing, even if you have accepted by telephone:

- State the position, the start date and the salary.
- Clarify any other benefits, such as relocation expenses.
- If you are relocating, ensure that you notify them of your new or interim contact details.
- Express your enthusiasm for the position and appreciation of the offer.

Declining a job offer

It is courteous to decline a job offer in writing. Be as positive and polite as possible – remember you may have dealings with the company, or the individuals who interviewed you, in the future:

- Express your appreciation of the offer.
- You do not need to go into detail about your decision, merely state that you have accepted another offer. (It is wise not to say that you have accepted a 'better offer'.)
- Thank any individual who was particularly helpful.
- End by wishing the company continued success.

ACCEPTANCE OF JOB OFFER

34 Woodbank
Tunbridge Wells
Kent
TN8 1WQ
Tel: 01892 456 789
Mobile: 0888 86666

Mr Simon Weir
Manager
Pilgrim's Rest
Chaucer Crescent
Canterbury
CT4 8UO

7 June 2005

ACCEPTANCE OF POSITION AS DUTY MANAGER

Dear Mr Weir

I am pleased to accept the position of Duty Manager at Pilgrim's Rest. I understand that my salary will be £13,500 and that I am to begin on Monday, 4 July 2005.

I look forward to working in Pilgrim's Rest and would like to thank you for giving me the opportunity to do so.

Yours sincerely

Robin Nicholson

Robin Nicholson

REJECTION OF JOB OFFER

5 Thackeray Terrace
Swansea
SA4 7OP
Tel: 01792 123 456
Mobile: 08888 44444

Mr Ieuan Morgan
Financial Controller
Dragon Technology Ltd
6 Bayside Enterprise Park
Swansea
SA9 8UY

8 August 2005

Assistant Accountant Position

Dear Mr Morgan

Thank you for your recent offer of a position as Assistant
Accountant.

However, after much careful consideration, I have now
decided to decline your offer and accept another position.

It was a pleasure meeting you and your team. Thank you for
the opportunity to learn more about Dragon Technology and
the position. I wish you and the company continued success.

Yours sincerely

Sarah Crockett

Sarah Crockett

Letters of resignation

Although resignation is done in person, a letter is almost always required for the record. Letters of resignation should be brief, but polite. Remember that you will probably need references from your employer, so refrain from the temptation to detail any grievances or voice any negative opinions. You may have to work with the company again in the future so leave on as positive a note as possible, even if the circumstances are difficult.

- Ensure that you give the correct amount of notice.
- Do not go into detail about your new position.
- Offer to make any transition as easy as possible.
- If you have to ask for a shorter notice period, do so as diplomatically as possible.
- Express your appreciation for any support or opportunities you have received within the company.

Useful phrases:

- I hereby tender my resignation from the firm, effective [date]
- As required by my contract of employment, I hereby give you 2 weeks' notice of my intention to leave my position as ...
- Circumstances require that I resign my position as [position], effective [date]
- After much consideration, I have accepted a position elsewhere.
- I have decided to return to full-time education/to change my career path.
- I would like to request that you waive my notice period/allow me to leave earlier.
- I will do all I can to aid the smooth transfer of my responsibilities before leaving.
- Please be assured that I will do everything in my power to enable a smooth transition ...
- If I may be of any assistance in training my successor/the recruitment process, I will gladly make myself available.
- I appreciate having had the opportunity of being a member of ...

- I would like to thank you for the experience I have gained while working for this company.
- I offer my best wishes for your continued success.
- I wish you and the company every success in the future.

LETTER OF RESIGNATION

148 Russell Avenue
Worsley
Manchester
M28 2SG
Tel: 0161 56789

Alison Farmer
Managing Director
Healthy Foods Ltd
Unit 7
Westcote Business Park
Salford
Greater Manchester
M5 6SS

19 September 2005

Dear Mrs Farmer

It is with regret that I submit this letter of resignation, effective 19 October 2005.

After much consideration, I have accepted a position elsewhere which will enable me to pursue my goals in the area of organic health management. As you are aware, this is an area that has been of interest to me for some time.

I will do everything I can to ensure that all projects are handed over smoothly. Please let me know if I can be of assistance in training my replacement.

It has been my pleasure to work for Healthy Foods Ltd for the past 4 years. I have enjoyed working with such professional colleagues and I wish you and the company continued success in the future.

Yours sincerely

Oliver Smeaton

Oliver Smeaton

Reservations

Travel and holiday reservations

Booking holidays

Making travel arrangements and booking accommodation is often done by telephone or through an agent. However, it is a good idea to confirm any telephone enquiry or booking in writing so that each person is clear about what is required or expected from the other.

These are some general points when making reservations in writing:

- Make sure you refer to the reason for writing as early as possible in order to alert the reader, either using a heading or in your opening sentence.
- Mention if you are responding to an advertisement or recommendation.
- If you are confirming a telephone booking in writing, all the details you have discussed and agreed with the hotel or guesthouse should be included in your letter of confirmation.
- If you are booking a package holiday, send a letter together with the booking form describing any special requirements you may have, and ask that the tour operator confirm in writing that the holiday will conform to all your requirements.
- Be as specific as you can about what you are asking for or agreeing to so that there can be no misunderstanding.

In your letter, it is important to specify the relevant details:

- Mention the number of rooms and beds you need. Be specific about details such as en suite bathroom, sea view, or whether you require a cot for a child or facilities for wheelchair users.
- Include the period of time you wish to stay. Give departure and arrival times where possible and specify days and dates. Be as clear as possible. If you are staying from the 4th to the 6th, does this mean that you are staying for two nights (and leaving on the morning of the 6th) or three nights (and leaving on the 7th)?
- State whether you are requesting bed and breakfast, half board or full board.
- Ask about the price or confirm the price agreed. Check whether a deposit is required.
- Include details of any special or unusual requirements you might have, such as dietary restrictions or disabled access, so that arrangements can be made well in advance.
- Ask for detailed directions or instructions on how to reach the hotel or guesthouse by road, rail, bus, etc.
- If you are driving to your accommodation, enquire whether there is parking available and, if so, whether a fee is required.

Booking a holiday on the Internet

The Internet is playing an increasingly important role in providing travel information. You can browse travel guides online and assess what is available in most parts of the world without having to wade through brochures or make repeated visits to the travel agent. In many cases it is possible to arrange your itinerary, book flights, train tickets and accommodation, and arrange car rental online.

E-mail correspondence is dealt with in more detail in Part 3. However, there are some points to bear in mind when booking a holiday on the Internet:

- It is necessary to confirm the details about dates, rooms, etc as specified above.
- Print out and keep copies of all correspondence, especially any confirmations of booking or payment.
- Make a note of any reference numbers, particularly for flights.
- It is often wise to check if the accommodation is approved by a tourist board or licensed by travel agents.
- If the booking has been made well in advance, it is often advisable to reconfirm the details by telephone before departure.

BOOKING A HOTEL ROOM

35 Daisy Hill
Long Eaton
Kent CT3 4LT
United Kingdom

The Manager
Harkers Lodge
467 Woodbridge Drive
HINTON AB TV7 7MX

June 13 2005

Dear Sir or Madam

Reservation for September

I saw your advertisement in this month's Country Pursuits. My wife and I will be travelling around Alberta in August and September. I would like to reserve a double room for the nights of 16, 17 and 18 September. Ideally, I would prefer a room with an en suite bathroom. Since my wife has difficulty climbing stairs, we will need a room situated either on the first floor or near a lift.

I would be grateful if you could let me know if you have a suitable room free on those dates. If so, please advise me of the total price to include breakfast (for three mornings). It would also be very helpful to us if you would forward details on how to get there by car. We would also be very grateful if you could forward us some information on local events and interesting places to visit in your area.

I look forward to hearing from you soon.

Yours faithfully

Alan Nixon

Alan Nixon

Other forms of reservation

When making or confirming other forms of reservations for events such as weddings, parties, or social functions, similar rules apply:

- If you are confirming a telephone booking in writing, all the details you have discussed should be included in your letter or e-mail of confirmation.
- Confirm dates, times and numbers.
- Be as specific as you can about what you are asking for or agreeing to.
- Include details of any special or unusual requirements you might have (such as dietary restrictions etc), so that arrangements can be made well in advance.
- Ask about the price or confirm the price agreed and check whether a deposit is required and how the full payment is to be made.
- Ask for detailed directions on how to reach the location by road, rail, bus, etc and check whether parking is available and if transport, such as taxis, can be arranged.

BOOKING A RESTAURANT FOR A FUNCTION

Alicia Chalmers
25 Seaview Avenue
St Ives
Cornwall
TR26 7SH

Tel: 01736 555566

Ms M Rahman
The Manager
The Rocky Lodge
2 Beechwood Road
Falmouth
Cornwall
FA5 8LC

17 November 2005

Dear Ms Rahman

Restaurant and Bar Reservation for 21 December 2005

Following our telephone conversation this morning, I am writing to confirm the reservation of your restaurant and bar facilities for the evening of 21 December.

There will be 200 guests in total for a four-course meal with wine. I look forward to receiving the menus you are sending and will inform you of our choices as soon as possible. I would appreciate written confirmation of the price agreed. I will then provide you with my credit card details so that a deposit can be paid.

Do not hesitate to contact me at the above telephone number if you need to discuss any further details.

Thanking you in advance.

Yours sincerely

Alicia Chalmers

Alicia Chalmers

Cancelling a reservation

When cancelling a reservation or booking, it is advisable to confirm it in writing, even if it has already been discussed by telephone.

Useful phrases:

- Unfortunately I must/have to cancel …
- I regret I must cancel …
- I understand that I am not entitled to the refund of my deposit of [amount].
- I would appreciate the refund of my deposit of [amount].
- Please accept my apologies for any inconvenience caused.
- I apologize for any inconvenience caused.

CANCELLING A RESERVATION

19 Silverbirch Park
Pitlochry
Tayside
PH16 5JS

Ms Hannah Maguire
Manager
Abbeyford Lodge Hotel
High St
Athenry
Co. Galway

17 November 2005

Dear Ms Maguire

Cancellation

As I informed you in our telephone conversation this morning, I regret I must cancel the reservation I made with you for a twin room for two nights from 19 to 21 December 2005.

I appreciate your refund of the deposit and I apologize for any inconvenience caused.

Yours sincerely

Angus McDougall

Angus McDougall

Invitations and replies

Formal invitations

There are two types of formal invitation: a printed card and a formal letter.

Printed cards

- Formal invitations on printed cards are always written in the third person and are traditionally printed in black.
- A standard card may be sent to all the prospective guests, or the cards may be personalized, with the guest's name written or printed on the card.
- There should be no date, opening greeting or complimentary close.
- The letters *RSVP* (an abbreviation of the French phrase *répondez s'il vous plaît*) meaning 'Please reply' are usually included. The invitation should include a response date by which time acceptances should be received, ideally no later than four weeks before the event. Some people prefer to include a printed response card.

Formal letters

A formal invitation in the form of a letter may be in the third person, or if slightly less formal, in the first and second persons. It should, of course, include an opening greeting and a complimentary close, but otherwise the information will be the same as for an invitation by printed card.

Informal invitations

Some people prefer to send a more informal invitation or letter. These need not be printed in black and can be personalized by incorporating drawings, photographs of the happy couple etc. A response is usually requested.

Remember to include the following information:

- The names of the bride and groom and the bride's parents or other hosts if it is a wedding invitation.
- Time, date, month and year of the event.
- Location of the venue.
- Address to which a reply should be sent.
- An informal invitation (to an event such as a wedding) may be handwritten or typed. If typed, the names of the invited guests should be added by hand.

Additional information

Remember to specify any additional requirements such as whether the event is black-tie or casual dress or whether children are invited.

Useful phrases

- … request the pleasure of your company
- … request the honour of your presence
- … would like you to join us in celebrating our engagement/anniversary/etc

PRINTED CARD (standard form to all guests)

Mr and Mrs Kenneth Jones

request the pleasure of your company
at the marriage of their daughter

Elizabeth Jane

to

Mr Edwin Forsyth

at Glasgow Cathedral
on Saturday 18th June 2006
at 2.30 p.m.
and afterwards at the reception at
The Craigard Hotel, Glasgow

RSVP
116 Cleveden Crescent
Glasgow GG1 0ZZ

PRINTED CARD (naming individual guests)

Mr and Mrs Kenneth Jones

request the pleasure of
the company of

[name(s) of guests]
at the marriage of their daughter

Elizabeth Jane
to
Mr Edwin Forsyth

at Glasgow Cathedral
on Saturday 18th June 2006
at 2.30 p.m.
and afterwards at the reception at
The Craigard Hotel, Glasgow

RSVP
116 Cleveden Crescent
Glasgow GG1 0ZZ

Nowadays, there are numerous ways of wording an invitation to reflect less traditional family arrangements.

INVITATION ISSUED BY THE DIVORCED PARENTS OF THE BRIDE

Mr. Angus Campbell and Mrs. Mary McLeod
request the pleasure of your company
at the marriage of their daughter
Mary Elizabeth Campbell...

INVITATION ISSUED BY THE REMARRIED MOTHER OF THE BRIDE AND HER HUSBAND

Mr. Simon & Mrs. Mary McLeod
request the pleasure of your company
on the occasion of
the marriage of Mrs. McLeod's daughter
Mary Elizabeth Campbell...

INVITATION ISSUED BY THE BRIDE AND GROOM

Miss Mary Elizabeth Campbell
and
Mr. Peter Greene
cordially invite you to
their marriage
at...

INFORMAL INVITATION

Aunt Rhian and Uncle Dai

James and I hope that you will be able to come to our wedding at Breedale Church, Blacksburgh, on Saturday 25th June at 1.30 p.m. The reception is at The Horse and Hound in Breedale Road. Please let us know if you will be able to come.

Love from

Silvia

91 Victoria Road
Cirencester
Gloucestershire
GL15 4JD

Replying to an invitation

- When replying to a formal invitation, whether accepting or declining the invitation, your reply should be handwritten, unless a response card has been included with the invitation.
- If the original invitation was in the third person you should also reply in the third person.
- There is no need to date or sign the reply.
- If you are declining a formal invitation you need only state that you are unable to attend – you are not required to give a reason.
- Replies to informal invitations can be in the form of a short handwritten note or letter.
- It is polite to reply to any invitation – formal or informal – as soon as possible, even if you are unable to attend.

Useful phrases

- Your kind invitation was received with sincere thanks.
- We would take great pleasure in attending ...
- It is with great pleasure that we accept your kind invitation to ...
- Unfortunately, we are unable to attend ...
- Unfortunately, we are unable to attend ... but wish you every happiness for the day.

ACCEPTANCE OF AN INVITATION (formal)

Mr and Mrs Armitage thank Mr and Mrs Fowler for their kind invitation to their daughter's wedding, and to the reception afterwards. They have much pleasure in accepting.

DECLINING AN INVITATION (formal)

We thank you for your kind invitation to your daughter's wedding, and to the reception afterwards, but regret that we are unable to attend.

ACCEPTANCE OF AN INVITATION (informal)

4 Maitland Street
CASPER WY 0538

July 13, 2005

Dear Mary-Lou,

Thanks so much for the invitation to your barbecue. I'll be delighted to come. It will be really good to see you all again.

Do you think I'll be able to get a bus from here? I'll phone you nearer the time to arrange the details. Meanwhile, let's hope the weather stays good for the barbecue! Thanks again for the invitation.

Look forward to seeing you soon.

Love,

Maria

Thank-you letters

Thank-you letters should be handwritten, and in most situations it is quite appropriate to use an informal conversational style of writing.

- When the thank-you letter is for a wedding, birthday, or Christmas present don't just write 'Thank you for the lovely present ...' You should mention what the present was, as in 'Thank you for the beautiful crystal wine glasses/fabulous pendant/book voucher ...' This will show that you know which present has been given by which person and avoid the impression that you are dashing off a whole series of standard thank-you letters simply because this is what is expected of you.
- Remember that the aim should be to convey your appreciation to the individual concerned, so personalize these letters as much as possible.
- Letters to work colleagues thanking them, for example, for a leaving gift or party should be written from your home address. The envelope should be addressed to the most senior member of staff and the letter itself to all the staff concerned.
- It is polite to write a thank-you note when you have been to someone's house for a formal dinner, or have been to stay with them. Similarly, if a business contact or acquaintance has entertained you to lunch or a trip to the theatre, this should be acknowledged in writing with your thanks. The thank-you letter should, of course, be sent as soon after the event as possible.

Useful phrases:

- I am writing to say thank you for ...
- I would like to thank you for ...
- I/We can't thank you enough for ...
- Thank you for your hospitality.
- ... for the hospitality you showed me and my wife/husband or to me.
- We were both delighted you could come ...
- It was really nice to see you at ...
- Give my thanks to ...
- Say thank you to ...

THANKS FOR A WEDDING PRESENT (before the event)

The Poplars
38 Skye Road
Ayr
KA1 9GX

18th April 2005

Dear Christine and Sandy,

Thank you very much for the beautiful crystal glasses you sent us as a wedding present. They will look wonderful on our dinner table and I intend to make good use of them.

It is lovely that you can both come to the wedding and we are very much looking forward to seeing you on the 21st.

I don't think John and I have ever been so busy, with all the organizing to do. There always seems to be something that still needs to be attended to!

We look forward to seeing you, and many thanks again.

With love,

Jenny and *John*

Jenny and John

THANKS FOR A WEDDING PRESENT (after the event)

167 Eccleshall Road
South Sheffield
S11 9PN

31st May 2005

Dear Sam and Lara,

We are writing to thank you for the lovely china vase you gave us as a wedding present. It looks fantastic in the hall and is just the right style for the house.

It was really nice to see you at the wedding – we had a wonderful day and it all seemed to run smoothly. Give my thanks to Tracey for the catering, everyone said how delicious the food was.

We had a lovely honeymoon in Thailand and are settling in well to the new house.

You must come and see us soon, and many thanks again.

With much love,

Sara and Dave

Sara and Dave

THANKS FOR HOSPITALITY

14 Westmorland Crescent
Whitecombe
Bedfordshire
SG16 7GB

12th October 2005

Dear Anne and Nigel,

We've just got back and I wanted to write to you immediately to tell you what a great weekend we had with you. Thanks a lot for inviting us – it was a real break for us both.

I didn't realize before that you lived so close to the sea – it was really relaxing going for walks along the beach. We especially enjoyed the meal in the pub on Sunday. It was a great little place, and the beer wasn't bad either.

I do hope we can come back and visit you again soon.

Remember, you're always welcome to come and stay with us any time. We have plenty of room here, and there are some interesting places we could visit.

Thanks again for putting us up, and keep in touch!

All the best,

Carol and *Mike*

Carol and Mike

THANKS FOR A DINNER PARTY

25 Paisley Lane
Liverpool
L5 9MO

12th November 2005

Dear Gareth and Karen,

That was a wonderful meal you gave us last night! Thank you so much. I must get that recipe for that fabulous chocolate cheesecake from you – although I'm not sure I will be able to make it as well as you did!

It was lovely to see Louise and Doug again, and chat about old times.

You must all come to us next time and we'll arrange something before Christmas, before everyone goes off on holiday.

With love,

Hazel

Sympathy and condolence

This chapter looks at letters expressing get-well wishes. It also deals with the difficult subject of death. It includes guidance on how to write letters informing people of a death as well as those expressing sympathy and condolence.

Illness

The tone and content of a letter expressing sympathy for an illness will depend very much on your relationship with the person and whether or not the illness is serious. When the condition, disease or injury is one from which the sufferer is likely to recover, the letter can be light and cheerful, even humorous. If you prefer, send a 'Get well soon' card with a short personal message. If the illness is more serious and it is known or suspected that recovery is unlikely, the approach needs to be somewhat different: misplaced optimism, detailed reference to the illness itself, or a bantering style may only cause further distress to the patient and their close relatives.

If you do send a letter, it should, preferably, be handwritten.

SYMPATHY TO THE RELATIVE OF AN ILL PERSON (formal)

> 10 Carr Avenue
> Halifax
> HX7 9QB
>
> 14 May 2005
>
> Dear Mrs Clitheroe,
>
> I was very sorry to hear of Mr Clitheroe's illness. Please give him my best wishes for a speedy recovery.
>
> Yours sincerely,
>
> Agnes Wright

SYMPATHY TO AN ILL PERSON (informal)

45 Rowan Crescent
Swansea
West Glamorgan
SA1 1RX

6 March 2005

Dear Rachel,

I was very sorry to hear from Marion that you have been taken ill so suddenly. Acute appendicitis is very painful and alarming. I wish I had known earlier and I would, of course, have visited you while you were in hospital. I'm very glad to hear that you are now back home and on the road to recovery. You'll need plenty of rest after your operation, but I'm sure Harry is making sure that you don't do too much too soon.

I'd like to come and visit later in the week. Let me know when would suit and if there is anything you need. I have some magazines that I think you might enjoy.

Take good care of yourself.

Best wishes,

Valerie

Letters of condolence

Death is said to be the last great taboo in Western society – we are not very good at dealing with it. Even those people who are most practised in the art of letter writing find letters of condolence amongst the most difficult to write. Many people shrink from the task for fear of intruding on the bereaved person's grief. The curious irony of this is that a grieving person's sense of loss and loneliness may be increased by the reserve or awkwardness of friends and acquaintances: being expected 'to get on with it' can prolong the grieving process, rather than shorten it. Sympathy and offers of support are comforting at any time of crisis or setback, but can be especially so when we have lost someone close to us. It is better to say something rather than nothing, and to feel embarrassed saying it rather than feeling awkward for not saying it. So try to put aside any fears you may have about doing 'the wrong thing' or 'finding the right words'. A simple and spontaneous acknowledgement of the loss suffered will almost always be appreciated and be of positive help to those most closely involved.

Many people choose to send a card with a short personal handwritten message inside. However, do take care with your choice of card. Pre-printed messages can seem a little impersonal and it is often better to avoid those that include stock phrases or overly-sentimental clichés. It is often better to write a proper letter.

The following points may help to guide you, especially if you have not had to write such a letter before.

- A letter or message of condolence should be handwritten.
- Formal letters of condolence to, for example, a business acquaintance, should always address the recipient by name.
- There is no need to include the address of the recipient.
- Try to use simple, straightforward, everyday language rather than anything more formal, flowery or poetic. Try not to use phrases like 'a blessed release' or 'a good innings'. Bear in mind the feelings of the person who will read the letter.

- Be sensitive to the reader's faith and spiritual beliefs in the language you use. Only refer to God or prayer if you know that the recipient of the letter shares your belief.
- Try to mention some aspect of the personality or character of the deceased (eg a love of sport or music, their ability to listen, their area of professional expertise) or to refer to some specific occasion or event for which you particularly remember them.

Useful phrases:
- It was with deep sadness that I/we heard of the death of ...
- I was/We were greatly saddened to learn of your wife's death.
- I/We wish to extend our deepest sympathy on your sad loss.
- I was/We were terribly upset to hear of ...
- I am writing to send you our warmest love and deepest sympathy.

LETTER OF CONDOLENCE TO A BUSINESS ACQUAINTANCE (formal style)

Arthur Jenkins Associates
Surveyors

25 Sycamore House
George St
Bath
BA2 5YU

Mr Thomas Grosvenor
Grosvenor & Cooper
31 Blenheim Crescent
Bath
BA3 9ZE

23 September 2005

Dear Mr Grosvenor

It was with deep sadness that I read of the sudden death of your business partner, Paul Cooper.

He will be greatly missed by the many clients who benefited from his professional advice over the years, and will be long remembered for the outstanding job he did on their behalf.

My staff join me in sending our sincere condolences and deepest sympathy to you and members of his family.

Yours sincerely

Arthur Jenkins

Arthur Jenkins
Jenkins and Paterson

LETTER OF CONDOLENCE TO A PERSONAL ACQUAINTANCE (formal style)

67 Hatchgate Way
Lower Kingcombe
Dorset
DT2 4LT

19 October 2005

Dear Mrs Halliway

My sister and I were very sad to hear of your husband's death last Tuesday, and I write to offer sincere condolences to you and your family.

I am sure you know how much Mr Halliway was liked and respected in the village, and was renowned for his encyclopedic knowledge of the locality. We will all miss him greatly.

If there is anything we can do to help, please do not hesitate to get in touch.

Kindest regards

Margaret and Emily

Margaret and Emily Chalmers

LETTER OF CONDOLENCE TO A FRIEND OR RELATIVE (informal style)

14 Trevelyan Close
Falmouth
Cornwall
TR5 8LC

February 3 2005

My dear David,

We were terribly sad to hear the tragic news of Barbara's death. It was a great shock, and we wanted you and the boys to know just how much you are all in our thoughts.

Barbara was loved by everyone who knew her, and we will treasure the memory of her warmth and kindness always.

You know that you can call on us at any time, and please don't hesitate if there is anything at all that we can do to help.

All our love and deepest sympathy,

Tom and *Anne*

Tom and Anne

LETTER INFORMING SOMEONE OF A DEATH

4 Didsbury Hill
Didsbury
MANCHESTER
M20 4KS

5 April 2005

Dear Mr Knight

I am very sorry to have to let you know that my father, John Murray, died in hospital on Monday.

As you may know, he had been ill for some time. He fought very bravely and it was only in the final few days that his condition deteriorated so much that he had to be admitted to hospital. He died peacefully in his sleep.

I know you and my father had been friends for many years, and he often talked with affection of the fishing trips you used to make together.

The funeral service is at 1.30 p.m. on Monday, 11th April at Minton Parish Church. We would be very pleased if you were also able to join us at my mother's house afterwards.

Yours sincerely

Brenda Murray

Brenda Murray

Part Three

E-mail

E-mail

E-mail

It is now common to use e-mail instead of letters as a means of personal communication, although for some more formal types of communication, a letter is still more appropriate.

> *Usage*
>
> It is important to think before you click on that 'Send' button – once an e-mail is sent, it is gone and cannot be stopped. Remember too, that e-mails remain on the hard drive and can be retrieved in the future.

Whether you use e-mail or traditional letters your aims are the same. You still need to think about presenting information clearly, so that the recipient gets the message and knows what is required. You also need to use language sensitively and strike an appropriate tone, so that you do not cause any unintentional offence.

> *i*
>
> Conventional letters sent by post are now often referred to as **snail mail**.

However, because e-mail is rapid and informal, and is always created using a computer keyboard, it has come to differ from the traditional letter in a few respects.

Addresses

E-mail addresses are made up of two parts, like this: *bennie@fast-deal.co.uk*. The first part of the name (before the @ symbol) is the user name; the second (after the @ symbol) is the **domain** and is usually the name of a company or organization ("fastdeal" in the example above), followed by a dot. This final part of the domain name can show the type of organization (eg **.com** or **.org**) and often also the country where the host server is located (eg **.com.au**).

An e-mail address is nearly always in lower-case lettering. Those e-mail addresses that do include upper-case letters in proper names have come to seem a bit 'fussy' and old-fashioned. Sometimes the use of spaces is avoided by using underscores:

> *raj@fishtank.co.uk*
> *marketing_dept@christmas.org*

It is important to type the exact address – get a single character wrong and the e-mail will not get through. Note also the address should be typed with no spaces between characters and no full stop at the end.

Headings

In order to send an e-mail, you need to state the address of the recipient(s) and your own address (this is usually generated automatically). These addresses are written in the heading at the top of an e-mail. If writing to more than one recipient, separate the addresses with a semicolon.

Usage

If you want to reply to a message received, there is no need to create a new message. Just click on the 'Reply' icon and type your
return message in the space that appears above the original (you
can choose whether or not to retain a copy of their message in your
reply). If the original message has been sent to more than one recipient, you can send your reply to all the others by clicking on 'Reply
All' – bear in mind who you want to read your reply!

The headings for e-mails are based on the headings of a traditional
memo (see page 56). In addition to the addresses of the recipient
and sender, you can also include other information in the heading:

- You can type in the addresses of other people to whom you
  wish to copy the e-mail. An address written in the line called *Cc:*
  (carbon copy) will be displayed at the top of the e-mail as a
  recipient of the message; an address written in the line called
  Bcc: (blind carbon copy) will be sent a copy of the message
  without being displayed at the top as a recipient.
- It is also customary to include a subject heading, indicating
  what your message is about. If you are replying to a previous e-
  mail, your mail tool will create the subject heading using *Re:*
  and the name of the previous e-mail.
- The heading is also the place where you can add attachments,
  other files that you wish to include as part of the message. You
  might include formal documents as attachments, with the e-
  mail itself acting as a cover note.

Attachments

E-mail allows you to attach graphics, word-processed, spreadsheet
and even program files to the message. You should first check with
the person to whom you are sending an attached file that they have
appropriate software that will allow them to open and read the
attachment.

> *Usage*
>
> Always check that you have attached the file before you click 'Send'.

Format of e-mails

E-mails can be sent in plain text or HTML format (and/or Rich Text). Plain text has no formatting, like this:

> The quick brown fox jumped over the lazy dog.

HTML (Hypertext Markup Language) is used to create web pages on the World Wide Web and offers the variety of type faces and sizes normally only available in word-processing programs; bold, italic and underlining; bullets and numbering in various styles; alignment and horizontal lines; and background styles. The Rich Text format has text formatting options, bullets and alignment. However, even if your e-mail program offers the options of HTML format and Rich Text format, you should always use plain text unless you are sure that the recipient of your message also has them as part of their software.

Beginning an e-mail

Because all the information that is necessary to send, receive and reply to e-mails is included in the headings, salutations and complimentary closes are not required but many people like to start messages with a greeting of some sort, even if it is only *hi*, *hello* or the first name of the person the message is being sent to.

- If you are sending a message to an address such as *admin@eazybank.co.ie* or to an online technical support service and do not know the name of the person you are writing to, opening with *hello* or *hi* is also perfectly acceptable.
- When writing a formal or business e-mail to somebody whom

you do not know very well, it is possible to use the format *Dear Mr/Mrs/Ms Green*. It is always best to err on the side of formality, particularly at the beginning of a correspondence. Be guided by their response or their 'signature'. If both first and surname are included, reply formally. If you know them, then it is more usual to simply use their first name.

- When writing to more than one person, it is possible to omit a greeting or to use one such as *Dear colleagues/Hello all/Hello everyone*, depending on the level of formality and the context. You can also refer to the group by their title, eg *Dear Members of the Committee*.

- When replying to a message from a colleague or friend, or from an online technical support service, it is common not to bother with such introductory greetings at all but simply to go straight into the main text of your reply.

Ending an e-mail

When answering messages from friends or colleagues, people will also often not bother to sign off the message, although you may prefer to do so. In any case, the most common ways of signing off an e-mail are much less formal than snail mail.

- Forms such as *Yours sincerely* are rarely used. Some people prefer to use less formal phrases, such as *Best wishes* or *Kind regards*.

- In the United States, business e-mails tend to be slightly more formal. *Sincerely* is often used for ending e-mails, especially to people who you don't know well. Others prefer to use the forms *All the best* and *Best regards* or, more informally, *Best* for ending a message.

- Friends and work colleagues use a variety of informal endings, such as *Talk later* or *Bye for now* (often abbreviated to *BFN*, see below). These endings may or may not be followed by the person's first name.

- Some people prefer to use an initial, eg 'P' for 'Peter'.

- It is also possible to add a 'signature' automatically to each e-mail you send. Your signature should include such details as your name, title, company name, address, telephone number and fax number. To create a signature click on your e-mail package's Tools menu and the Mail Format option, or its equivalent.

Writing style for e-mail messages

Because it can be sent quickly and casually, e-mail correspondence tends to be fairly informal in style. An e-mail is more like a note than a formal letter, which takes time to be composed, written, posted and delivered.

Some people almost exclusively use lower case when writing e-mail. The logic for this lies in the quick and casual nature of e-mail, mentioned above, which militates against the unnecessary extra effort required to hold down the shift key to create capitals. The principle of reducing unnecessary effort can also lead in other directions:

- E-mail tends to use a lot of abbreviations and acronyms, some of which are listed below.
- Writers of e-mail are often less fussy about correcting of spelling mistakes when keying at high speed.
- There is less use of apostrophes and more subtle punctuation. Colons and semicolons are often replaced by dashes.
- As underlining usually indicates a link to a website, it is not used to add emphasis. Some people add the equivalent of spoken emphasis to a word or words in their e-mail by enclosing the words to be emphasized in asterisks, eg 'You *really* mustn't miss this film.'

However, if you are unsure about which style to use in an e-mail, and particularly if the message is important, it is best to use a more formal style as it will generally not cause offence. If the person replies in a more informal style, you may follow that style in your next message.

E-mail etiquette, or netiquette

Although e-mail is more informal than letter writing, you should still be sensitive to what is and is not appropriate, especially with people you do not know. In addition, you still need to be clear about what you are saying: inconsistent or incorrect language can be open to misinterpretation. It is worth putting a little thought into the composition of your message, especially if it is being sent in plain text format, which does not allow formatting such as bold or italic. While you may intend it to be read in a particular way, this may not always be apparent to the reader.

People writing e-mails are expected to observe a code of behaviour known as **netiquette**. If you follow a few basic rules you will avoid annoying or offending the people you write to and thus communicate effectively with them.

- Clearly summarize the contents of your message in the subject line. This makes it easier for people to sort and prioritize their mail.
- Keep your messages short and to the point. This is particularly true in a business environment.
- Avoid writing your whole message in capital letters. It is harder to read and THE READER WILL OFTEN PERCEIVE IT AS SHOUTING.
- Do not overquote previous messages in your replies. When responding to a message, you can include the text of the message you are replying to in your answer by using the 'Reply' function. You should only quote the parts of the previous message or messages that are relevant to your response. These can be interspersed with your replies, point by point.
- Use emoticons (see below) with care. Smileys should only be used in personal e-mail and not for business or, as a rule, in the office. It is best to stick to using smileys to convey a particular tone of voice, ie to give a particular emphasis to what you have said. It is considered rude to write something derogatory followed by a winking smiley to imply that you don't mean it seriously.

- Do not overuse abbreviations and acronyms (see below). Not everyone is familiar with abbreviations like *BTW* ('by the way') and people may be reluctant to admit that they don't understand them. It is best only to use abbreviations when writing to people who you know to be conversant with them.
- Avoid sarcasm and irony unless the recipient is familiar with your style.
- Do not make defamatory, libellous or offensive comments about people, groups or organizations in e-mail messages: you may find yourself on the wrong end of a lawsuit.
- Do not attach large files without the recipient's prior permission. Most email servers will not accept attachments larger than 10Mb (10,000Kb). Many e-mail accounts have quotas. Be especially aware when sending attachments to webmail accounts as they tend to have very low quotas. Also be aware of sending large attachments to someone who is on holiday. You may put someone's account over quota, and thus stop them from receiving e-mail until they return.
- Only send messages to people for whom they are really relevant rather than using the *Carbon Copy* (*Cc*) function to copy them to everyone.
- If you are sending a message to a group of people who may not all know each other, use *Blind Carbon Copy* (*Bcc*) to avoid giving people's addresses to those whom they do not know.
- Never forward e-mail to other people without permission.

Abbreviations used in e-mail

It is customary to use many abbreviations in informal e-mail. These often take the form of a common expression being represented only by the initial letters of the words. Many of these are now used routinely, although it is a good idea to make sure those you send messages to are familiar with these before you start to include them in your messages.

Here are some of the more common abbreviations encountered in e-mail:

abbreviation	meaning
AFAIK	as far as I know
AFK	away from keyboard
ASAP	as soon as possible
ATB	all the best
B4	before
BAK	back at keyboard
BBL	be back later
BTDT	been there done that
BTW	by the way
CLD	could
CUL8R	see you later
F2F	face to face
FAQ	frequently asked question
FYI	for your information
GAL	get a life
GTG	got to go
HTH	hope this helps
IMHO	in my humble opinion
IMO	in my opinion
IOW	in other words
L8	late
L8R	later
LOL	laughing out loud (when someone has written something funny)
MSG	message
MYOB	mind your own business
NE1	anyone
NRN	no reply necessary
NW!	no way!
OMG	Oh my God!
OTOH	on the other hand
PLS	please

POV	point of view
TBD	to be discussed
THRU	through
TIA	thanks in advance
TNX	thanks
TTYL	talk to you later
TVM	thanks very much
WRT	with regard to
XOXOXO	hugs and kisses

Emoticons and smileys

Another convention used by e-mailers is the use of **emoticons** (also called **smileys**). These are combinations of keyboard characters – mainly punctuation marks – that are used to show facial expressions and emotions. Emoticons are invariably used in informal e-mails. Here are some examples of the more commonly used ones:

Emoticon		**Emoticon**	
:-)	happy	:-C	really upset
:-))	really happy	:-O	surprised
:-D	laughing out loud	:-@	screaming
:-(	sad	8-)	glasses
;-)	wink	|-)	sleep
:-((	really sad	:-/	undecided
:´-(	crying	d:-)	baseball cap
:-|	frowning	|-O	yawn
:-||	really angry	:-*	kiss

Security

There are precautions you can take to make e-mail correspondence more secure:

- Do not send highly sensitive information (such as credit card numbers or PINs) by e-mail.
- Be sure to have good anti-virus software.
- Viruses are usually spread in attachments. Be wary of attachments that you were not expecting. Do not open attachments from people who you do not know.
- Attached files should only be saved to your hard disk if you run a virus check on the file attachment before saving.
- It is good practice to zip any attachments you send. It not only makes them smaller, but also can protect files from corruption in transit.

E-MAIL TO A FRIEND

E-mails among friends can take any form. They are frequently tele-graphic in style, using abbreviations and emoticons.

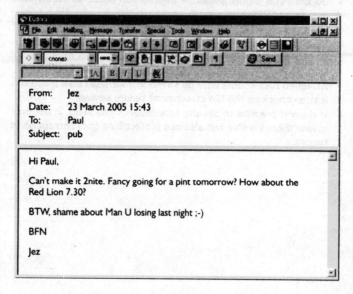

E-MAIL TO AN UNKNOWN RECIPIENT

Since in this case the name of the recipient is unknown, the message simply begins with *Hi*. Note that this informal opening is preferred to the more formal openings such as *Dear Sir/Madam* used in snail mail. The message is to the point, providing as much information as necessary for the problem to be properly understood, and the problem is summarized clearly in the subject line. It is polite to end messages requesting help with *Thanks*.

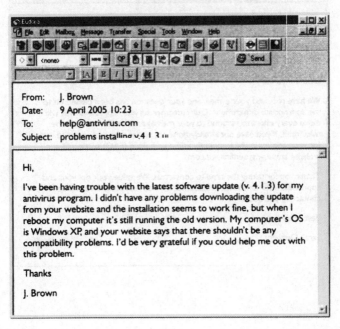

From: J. Brown
Date: 9 April 2005 10:23
To: help@antivirus.com
Subject: problems installing v.4.1.3 ...

Hi,

I've been having trouble with the latest software update (v. 4.1.3) for my antivirus program. I didn't have any problems downloading the update from your website and the installation seems to work fine, but when I reboot my computer it's still running the old version. My computer's OS is Windows XP, and your website says that there shouldn't be any compatibility problems. I'd be very grateful if you could help me out with this problem.

Thanks

J. Brown

E-MAIL RESPONDING TO A CUSTOMER ENQUIRY

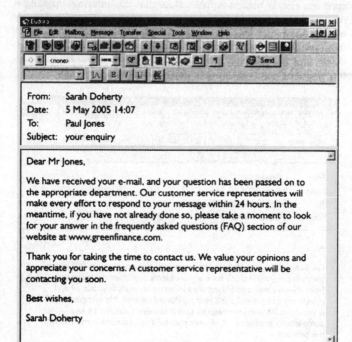

From: Sarah Doherty
Date: 5 May 2005 14:07
To: Paul Jones
Subject: your enquiry

Dear Mr Jones,

We have received your e-mail, and your question has been passed on to the appropriate department. Our customer service representatives will make every effort to respond to your message within 24 hours. In the meantime, if you have not already done so, please take a moment to look for your answer in the frequently asked questions (FAQ) section of our website at www.greenfinance.com.

Thank you for taking the time to contact us. We value your opinions and appreciate your concerns. A customer service representative will be contacting you soon.

Best wishes,

Sarah Doherty

E-MAIL QUERY AND RESPONSE BETWEEN BUSINESS COLLEAGUES WHO KNOW EACH OTHER QUITE WELL

As in the e-mail between friends, informal openings and endings are used, but note the absence of smileys and abbreviations, since this is mainly a work message rather than a personal one. The first line of each message is more personal, and consequently the style for this part is more telegraphic than the business part of the message.

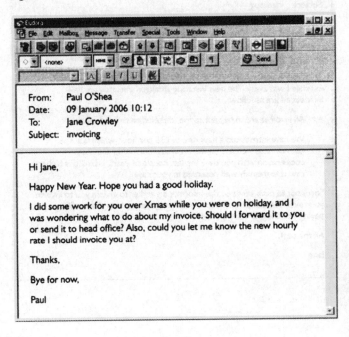

From: Paul O'Shea
Date: 09 January 2006 10:12
To: Jane Crowley
Subject: invoicing

Hi Jane,

Happy New Year. Hope you had a good holiday.

I did some work for you over Xmas while you were on holiday, and I was wondering what to do about my invoice. Should I forward it to you or send it to head office? Also, could you let me know the new hourly rate I should invoice you at?

Thanks,

Bye for now,

Paul

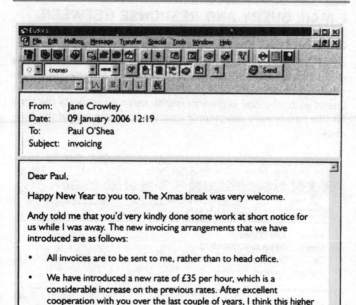

From: Jane Crowley
Date: 09 January 2006 12:19
To: Paul O'Shea
Subject: invoicing

Dear Paul,

Happy New Year to you too. The Xmas break was very welcome.

Andy told me that you'd very kindly done some work at short notice for us while I was away. The new invoicing arrangements that we have introduced are as follows:

- All invoices are to be sent to me, rather than to head office.

- We have introduced a new rate of £35 per hour, which is a considerable increase on the previous rates. After excellent cooperation with you over the last couple of years, I think this higher rate is extremely well deserved in your case.

Sorry not to have sent you this information earlier to enable you to invoice your most recent work. I'm sure you'll be happy to hear that we'll be paying you a higher rate in future.

All the best,

Jane

FORMAL MESSAGE TO A BUSINESS CONTACT

The style of this e-mail is similar to that of an equivalent traditional letter. However, it closes with the less formal *With best wishes* rather than *Yours sincerely*. Bear in mind that this more formal type of e-mail is often retained for the company's records, and so may be regarded as an official and permanent record of communication, like a letter.

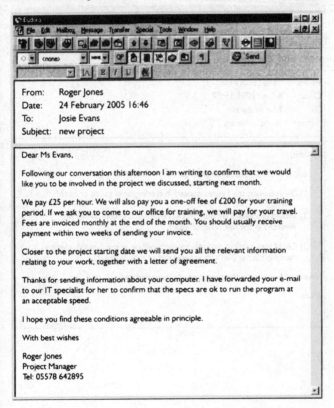

From: Roger Jones
Date: 24 February 2005 16:46
To: Josie Evans
Subject: new project

Dear Ms Evans,

Following our conversation this afternoon I am writing to confirm that we would like you to be involved in the project we discussed, starting next month.

We pay £25 per hour. We will also pay you a one-off fee of £200 for your training period. If we ask you to come to our office for training, we will pay for your travel. Fees are invoiced monthly at the end of the month. You should usually receive payment within two weeks of sending your invoice.

Closer to the project starting date we will send you all the relevant information relating to your work, together with a letter of agreement.

Thanks for sending information about your computer. I have forwarded your e-mail to our IT specialist for her to confirm that the specs are ok to run the program at an acceptable speed.

I hope you find these conditions agreeable in principle.

With best wishes

Roger Jones
Project Manager
Tel: 05578 642895

QUERY AND RESPONSE BETWEEN EMPLOYEE AND MANAGER

In this exchange, the questions and answers are brief and to the point. Note that in the response, the introductory lines of the message have been deleted, as they are not necessary for the email.

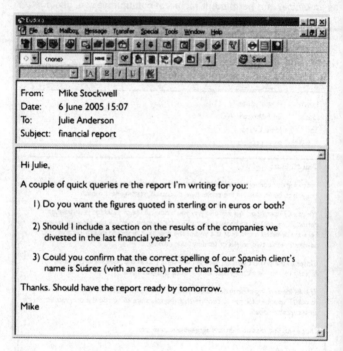

From: Mike Stockwell
Date: 6 June 2005 15:07
To: Julie Anderson
Subject: financial report

Hi Julie,

A couple of quick queries re the report I'm writing for you:

   1) Do you want the figures quoted in sterling or in euros or both?

   2) Should I include a section on the results of the companies we divested in the last financial year?

   3) Could you confirm that the correct spelling of our Spanish client's name is Suárez (with an accent) rather than Suarez?

Thanks. Should have the report ready by tomorrow.

Mike

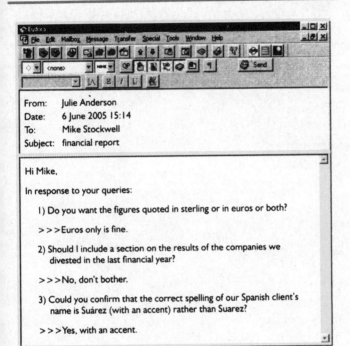

Supplement

Grammar, punctuation and spelling

The odd instance of bad grammar, misspelling or poor punctuation may go unnoticed in a personal letter. However, in formal and business letters and e-mail your aim should be to get your message across clearly and unambiguously, and the structure of your sentences should reflect this aim.

Grammar

Here are some of the more important grammar rules that you might want to keep in mind as you write.

Use active rather than passive verbs:

- ✗ *It was agreed by the committee that further amendments to the law were necessary.*

- ✔ *The committee agreed that further amendments to the law were necessary.*

Try to keep to the same tense (ie past, present or future):

- ✗ *When I received your order, I pass it to the relevant department.*

- ✔ *When I received your order, I passed it to the relevant department.*

Verbs should agree with their subject in person (*I go, he goes*) and number (*She goes, they go*):

- ✗ *I agrees that the client should be notified as soon as the problems is solved.*

✓ *I agree that the client should be notified as soon as the problems are solved.*

Verbs that link information to the subject, such as *seem*, *appear* and *be*, should also agree with the subject in number. In the following example, the verb *be* must be in singular ('is') even if the extra information ('expenses') is in the plural:

✗ *Our main concern are our expenses.*

✓ *Our main concern <u>is</u> our expenses.*

When the subject is plural ('overheads') and the extra information ('problem') is singular the verb should be in the plural:

✗ *Our overheads is a problem.*

✓ *Our overheads <u>are</u> a problem.*

Avoid double negatives:

✗ *I never knew no greater joy.*

✓ *I never knew greater joy.*

Avoid double comparatives and double superlatives:

✗ *It was much more quicker than I expected.*

✓ *It was much quicker than I expected.*

Try to avoid splitting too many infinitives (ie inserting a word between *to* and a following verb), though this is not strictly ungrammatical:

✗ *He started to gradually realize his mistake.*

✓ *He gradually started to realize his mistake.*

To avoid ambiguity in writing, the words *even* and *only* should be placed as closely as possible to the word or words they are intended to emphasize. Notice the effect that putting *even* and *only* in different places has on the meaning in the following examples:

> *Even I had washed the floor.*
> [= It was unusual for me to wash the floor.]
>
> *I had even washed the floor.*
> [= I had washed the floor as well as sweeping it.]
>
> *I had washed even the floor.*
> [= I had washed everything including the floor.]
>
> *Only the managers need to attend.*
> [=Nobody besides the managers needs to attend.]
>
> *The managers only need to attend.*
> [= The managers do not have to do anything except attend.]

Take care not to use a 'dangling participle':

> ✗ *Driving along a country road last week, a tree fell on our car.*

This wording suggests that the tree was driving. Rephrase the sentence:

> ✔ *As we were driving along a country road last week, a tree fell on our car.*

Avoid the omission of the preposition that always accompanies a particular verb:

> ✗ *I was dreaming and hoping for a long break.*
>
> ✔ *I was dreaming of and hoping for a long break.*

I is used before the verb when you are part of the subject, even when other people are included:

> ✗ *Me and Jane like gardening.*

> ✓ *Jane and I like gardening.*

Use *me* after a verb, eg *he gave me a lift home.* However, it is a common error to use *I* instead of *me* when other people are included, eg:

> ✗ *She gave Alan and I a lift home.*

> ✓ *She gave Alan and me a lift home.*

Another common error is to use *I* instead of *me* after a preposition, eg:

> ✗ *William waved to Anne and I as he drove away.*

> ✓ *William waved to Anne and me as he drove away.*

Usage

If in doubt, try out the construction you want to use but omitting everything except 'me' or 'I'. A mistake will be obvious.

✗ *William waved to I as he drove away.*

Punctuation

Letters are nowadays usually typed in blocked style with 'open punctuation': that is, with the minimum punctuation required for clarity. This applies in the addresses, the main text of the letter and other elements in the letter, such as the salutation, heading and complimentary close.

The punctuation of other elements in a letter

In business and official letters, a colon is used in various conventional elements that are outside the main text of the letter. These include the reference line or lines, the attention line, and in a subject heading made up of two parts.

Our reference: LW03/KMC
Your reference: KB/MM
For the Attention of: Dr Isabel Stewart
Expenses: new claim forms
Account number: X00000

> **i**
>
> In American texts a colon is used after the initial greeting in a letter (***Dear Sir:***) where in British English there would be a comma (***Dear Sir,***).

Punctuation in the main text of the letter

The punctuation of the main text of your letter should follow the rules that apply to any piece of writing.

Full sentences

Begin each sentence with a capital letter and end it with a full stop, a question mark or an exclamation mark. A full stop is used at the end of a sentence that is a statement, a question mark at the end of a sentence that is a question, and an exclamation mark at the end of an interjection, an exclamation or a command.

> *Usage*
>
> Do not forget to insert a question mark at the end of a question.

Comma

A comma is usually used for lists, separating clauses and after adverbs, such as *however*, that link a sentence to a previous one.

A pair of commas is used to enclose extra information or a commenting word or phrase in the middle of a sentence, eg *He arrived, I kid you not, wearing a tutu*.

> **Usage**
>
> Remember to include the second enclosing comma. It is a common error to omit it, especially if the clause to be enclosed is a long one.

Apostrophe

An apostrophe is used to create the possessive form of nouns eg *the man's hat*. Apostrophes are also used in contracted forms at the point where one letter is, or several letters are, omitted: *they've, he's, we're, hadn't*.

> **Usage**
>
> Remember that *it's* (with an apostrophe) is the short form of *it is*. The possessive form has no apostrophe, eg *its back bumper*.

✗ *potatoe's and carrot's*

The apostrophe should not be used to make plurals, except to clarify plurals of some short words, as in *dot the i's and cross the t's*.

Colon and semicolon

A colon is used to indicate that what follows explains, expands on or completes the part that has gone before. What follows the colon may be a complete sentence, a list or even a single word:

> *There's a classic film on at the local cinema: Vertigo, I think.*

A semicolon is used instead of a word like 'and' or 'but' to separate two clauses of equal importance, if one part balances or contrasts with the other: *He made another dive for the ball; he missed again*. Semicolons are also used to separate groups of items in a complex list, often one where individual items are separated by commas.

Note the difference in meaning that the two marks can create. The semicolon in the following sentence suggests that the two statements are balanced, and Frankie's laughter and Jim's embarrassment both arise independently from the same source:

> *Frankie laughed hysterically; Jim was turning purple with embarrassment.*

But if a colon is used, the second statement should be read as an explanation of the first, with the implication that Frankie's laughter arises from Jim's embarrassment:

> *Frankie laughed hysterically: Jim was turning purple with embarrassment.*

Brackets, dashes or commas?

> i
>
> Extra information that is inserted into a sentence that is already complete in itself is called a **parenthesis** or **parenthetic information**.

When you want to mark off 'parenthetic' information within a sentence, you can use brackets, dashes or commas. The choice depends on how much you want to distance the parenthetic information from the rest of the sentence.

Brackets are the strongest way to mark off parenthetic information. They are used around information that is less important than the surrounding sentence. Words inside brackets do not have to flow as smoothly from what went before as words enclosed by dashes or commas:

> *Camping (not everyone's cup of tea) is a relatively inexpensive option.*

Dashes also represent a strong break, often suggesting a change in emphasis or tone from the surrounding sentence. However, they are not as strong as brackets, and the words inside the dashes should flow on smoothly from what went before:

> *Camping is a relatively inexpensive – albeit less comfortable – option.*

Commas are the weakest form of punctuation for parenthetic information. The words enclosed by commas are not cut off as distinctly from the surrounding sentence:

> *Camping is, as you might expect, a relatively inexpensive option.*

Spelling

Bad spelling will not only distract the reader from the content of your letter or e-mail, but will give the message that you have not taken the trouble to get it right.

- If you are unsure of the spelling of a word, check it first in a dictionary.
- If you are having your letter typed by someone else, always check it for errors before you sign it.
- Remember that spellchecks in word-processing programs are not infallible and are unlikely to recognize proper names or technical terms. They do not help if you have used the wrong word, but have spelled it properly.
- It is important, for courtesy's sake, to spell the name of the recipient correctly, and to get their job title right.

Spelling checklists

Words ending in **-able** and **-ible** are frequently misspelled, often because the endings can sound similar when spoken. Some words can be spelled with either ending. Use the checklist below for easy reference.

accessible	gullible	preferable
advisable	horrible	preventable/
agreeable	hospitable	preventible
amicable	indefensible	probable
applicable	indestructible	reliable
capable	inevitable	reprehensible
changeable	inexcusable	respectable
collectable/	inexhaustible	responsible
collectible	inflexible	reversible
communicable	intolerable	saleable
compatible	irrepressible	sensible
culpable	irresistible	sociable
despicable	knowledgeable	susceptible
detachable	lamentable	tangible
detectable/	legible	terrible
detectible	memorable	unforgettable
detestable	negligible	unforgivable
edible	noticeable	unmistakable
eligible	payable	unstoppable
fashionable	peaceable	usable/useable
fallible	perceptible	variable
feasible	permissible	viable
flexible	plausible	visible
forcible	portable	vulnerable
formidable	possible	
foreseeable	predictable	

Here are some more words that are frequently misspelled or whose spellings can be confused. Bear in mind that some words may be spelled differently in American English.

abandoned	absent	accidentally
absence	accept	accommodation

accuracy
accurate
achieve
acknowledge
acquaintance
acquire
across
address
advice *(noun)*
advise *(verb)*
affect *(verb)*/effect
  (noun)
answer
apology
apologize
apparently
appearance
appreciate
argument
assess
assist
assistance
assistant
attach
attachment
autumn
awful
awfully
baggage
beautiful
beginner
beginning
behaviour

believe
breadth
Britain
brochure
business
calendar
cancel
cancelled
cancelling
cancellation
career
careful
carefully
catalogue
category
colleague
commit
commitment
committed
committing
comparative
concede
connection
convenience
correspondence
courteous
deceive
December
decide
decision
decisive
definite
definitely

deliberate
dependant *(noun)*
dependent
  (adjective)
describe
develop
developed
developing
difference
disappear
disappoint
disapprove
discrepancy
dispatch or
  despatch
dissatisfied
eighth
embarrass
embarrassment
enclosed
enclosure
envelope
equipped
especially
etc (et cetera)
excellent
exciting
exhibition
experience
extraordinary
extremely
favourite
February

financial	language	personnel
finish	leisure	persuade
foreign	liaise	piece
foreigner	liaison	planning
friend	licence *(noun)*	possess
fulfil	license *(verb)*	possibility
gauge	maintenance	practice *(noun)*
government	manoeuvre	practise *(verb)*
grateful	marriage	prefer
grief	medicine	preferred
grieve	message	preparation
guarantee	messenger	principal
guard	mortgage	principle *(noun)*
guess	necessary	privilege
guide	neither	probably
happened	niece	pronounce
happening	ninth	pronunciation
height	nuisance	pursue
honorary	occasionally	receipt
honourable	occur	receive
humorous	occurred	recommend
humour	occurring	reference
immediately	omit	refer
inaccurate	omission	referred
incidentally	opportunity	referring
independent	opposite	referral
install	ordinary	repetition
installation	passenger	resign
instalment	permanent	satisfactory
intelligence	permit	schedule
interrupt	permitted	scheme
journey	permitting	sentence
knowledge	personal	separate

sign	sympathy	**Tuesday**
similar	technical	twelfth
sincerely	temporary	unfortunately
skilful	thorough	unnecessary
stopped	through	vehicle
stopping	travel	**Wednesday**
succeed	travelled	whole
suddenness	travelling	wholly

Vocabulary and style

It is important that your letters and e-mails are clear, coherent and correct. This chapter includes some guidance on appropriate vocabulary and style.

Choosing the right vocabulary and having a straightforward style can make your letters and e-mails easier to read and more effective. Use the following principles to develop your writing style:

- Write in the appropriate form of English.
- Express yourself clearly.
- Eliminate unnecessary words and avoid repetition.
- Use language sensitively.

Write in the appropriate form of English

As discussed previously, you have to bear in mind your reader and the occasion or context. Should the language be formal, slangy, informal or technical? The language you use for a chatty letter to an old friend will be very different to that required for a technical e-mail to a colleague. Avoid jargon unless you are communicating with someone who you know is familiar with the terminology. Once you have decided on the correct form, be consistent and do not waver between formal and informal language.

Writers of business letters, in particular, often fall into the trap of using formulaic expressions to create what they imagine is a suitably detached and business-like tone. However, many of these expressions are nowadays regarded as relics of a bygone age or just plain pompous. It is always better to keep it simple and clear.

Express yourself clearly

Your readers should not have to work too hard to interpret your writing. You can help your reader by using language precisely and avoiding overused words such as *nice*, *bad* or *good*.

Try to be aware of ambiguity and nuances. Many English words have several different meanings or connotations, and so careless writing can easily lead to misunderstanding. Some words are neutral while others betray your subjective opinion. To describe something as *reasonable* or *affordable* is quite positive; on the other hand *cheap* or *cut-rate* are more pejorative. *Intelligent* or *bright* are fairly positive terms, while *shrewd* or *cunning* imply an underhand element to someone's smartness and so often sound unfavourable.

Keep your paragraphs short and to the point. Avoid complicated sentence structures. If a sentence runs to more than 30 words it can probably be split up into two shorter sentences. If you have to use longer sentences, use conjunctions such as *neither... nor...* or *not only ... but also ...* to impose a clear structure and indicate the train of thought.

Do not use words when you are not completely sure what they mean, and don't use difficult words merely for the sake of it. Try to get your message across using plain English: most everyday words are as appropriate in formal contexts as in informal ones. Ask yourself if it is necessary to use, for example, *purchase* instead of *buy*, *endeavour* instead of *try*, or *commence* instead of *start*. More often than not, the more familiar word will do the job just as well or probably better.

Follow the rules of spelling and grammar (see previous chapter).

Eliminate unnecessary words and avoid repetition

One of the best ways of expressing yourself clearly is to watch out for words that do not contribute anything to the meaning of a sentence. You may be able to simplify your writing by removing unnecessary words and phrases, or by using one word instead of several.

Rewrite clichés

Many clichéd phrases can be written in simpler terms:

phrase	simple form
and also	and
as to whether	whether
at your earliest convenience	as soon as possible/as soon as is convenient
consequent upon	after
the reason is because	the reason is
because of the fact that	because
by virtue of the fact that	because
due to the fact that	because
in the event that	if
at this moment in time	now
on a daily basis	daily
with a view to	to
is located	is
enclosed herewith	enclosed *or simply* I enclose
in the course of	during
Re your letter of ...	I/We refer to your letter of ...

Eliminate redundant phrases

Similarly, certain expressions often add nothing to the meaning of a sentence. Eliminate the following phrases if the sentence can stand up without them:

> *when all is said and done*
> *in actual fact*
> *as a matter of fact*
> *in point of fact*
> *at the end of the day*
> *not to put too fine a point on it*
> *in a very real sense*
> *basically*
> *actually*

Eliminate old-fashioned phrases

Avoid phrases that are too vague, pompous or difficult to understand, such as Latin abbreviations:

> *a copy of the same*
> *inst., prox., ult.*
> *in early course*
> *yours to hand*

Omit intensifiers

Intensifiers, such as *really*, *very*, *quite* and *extremely*, are also often superfluous.

Avoid saying the same thing twice

Tautology is a fault in style in which a word (or a group of words) is added, unnecessarily repeating the meaning of a word (or words) already used in the phrase or sentence. The underlined words in the following sentences could and should be eliminated, because the idea they express is already present:

> We must insist that immediate payment of all outstand-
> ing sums is made <u>forthwith</u>.
>
> Please refer to the documents enclosed <u>herewith</u>.
>
> We progressed <u>forward</u> slowly.

Usage

Do not use *again* after a word that begins with the prefix *re-*. The
idea of repetition is already present in the prefix, and so *again* is
redundant.

Use language sensitively

Your aim should be to establish and keep up a good relationship
with your reader. You want them to trust you and listen to your
message. Often you want them to be persuaded by your argument
or act in accordance with your request or recommendation.

The last thing that you want to do is to ruin this relationship by
writing in a way that irritates or offends the reader. Be aware of
words that may be regarded as taboo or offensive.

Language is most likely to be considered as offensive or derogatory when it implies a judgement about other individuals or about
groups to which other individuals belong. Sensitive areas include
gender, nationality/race, religion and physical or mental capability.

Sensitive use of language is a complicated and emotive area. There
are no fixed rules about what is acceptable and what is inappropri-
ate, and people often disagree. However, the following general
principles may be helpful:

- Some traditional ways of referring to people may reinforce ideas
  that are unhelpful and are often incorrect, for example with
  regard to the roles of men and women in society or the lifestyles
  and values of ethnic minority groups.

- On the other hand, well-intentioned attempts to avoid insensitive language can sometimes interfere with the clear or direct expression of meaning, and can appear ridiculous if taken to extremes.
- People usually prefer to be regarded as individuals rather than as members of a particular group, and often it is not relevant to refer to people's race, gender or physical capability.
- There are often differences between the ways people refer to themselves, and the ways that they like to be referred to by others. It is a good idea to respect the right of people to choose how they should be referred to. Bear in mind that a group may use a term itself, but might still regard this term as offensive when applied to it by others.
- Ideas about what is appropriate might vary from country to country or region to region, and also change over time, so that terms that were at one time considered acceptable might now be regarded as offensive.

Writing on-screen

Word-processing packages often come as part of the software 'suite' supplied with new personal computers. Writing on-screen does away with the need for carbon copies – the letter can be saved to your hard disk, or an extra copy printed for your files.

As well as producing a well-finished, professional-looking final result, word-processing programs also have a number of functions that can make life easier when working with text:

- **Font type and size** allows you to vary the size of your typeface. In business contexts, and particularly for CVs, it is better to stick to typefaces such as Arial or Times New Roman. Use a size of not less than 11 point.
- **Copy and paste** allows you to duplicate any area of your text quickly and simply, so that if a heading or passage needs to be repeated you can make sure it appears in exactly the same way each time. It is also useful if you want to write a passage that differs only slightly from something you have already written. Simply copy and paste the first passage, and then alter it to produce the second.
- **Undo** and **redo** changes material and changes it back, so you can compare different versions of your work or undo errors – for example, if you have deleted or changed material by mistake.
- **Find and replace** locates every instance of a particular word or phrase and allows you to replace it with another. This can be useful for ensuring that your work is consistent and allows you to deal with all occurrences of a particular error at once. For example, it will enable you find every occurrence of the word *Peking* and change them all to *Beijing*. You need to be careful, however, that you do not accidentally change something that

you really wanted to leave unaltered (for example, you would not want to change *Peking duck* to *Beijing duck*). Another pitfall of this feature is that it can create changes to the layout of the text without you being aware of it. For example, the amount of text on a line or on a page may be altered.

- **Autocorrection** is a feature that detects errors and makes changes without the need for you to do anything. Bear in mind that sometimes you might wish to write something that the computer has been programmed to change.

- **Wizards** are short-cut features that bring together all the standard commands required to perform a series of tasks. They can be used for laying out and formatting documents such as letters, CVs, faxes and memos. While they may sometimes be too formulaic for your particular requirements, they can be useful tools for giving ideas and hints.

Address book

The electronic address book is a useful feature that can be shared by the various applications in your computer. You need only type a person's details (name, job title, company name, postal address, e-mail address, fax number, telephone number) into the address book once. Thereafter, select a name in the address book using the mouse, and the computer will extract appropriate details for whichever means of communication you are using: name and address to be added to a letter, e-mail address for a new message, fax number for the fax cover page, or telephone number for automatic dialling.

Standard or form letters

If you regularly use standard letters to send to clients, customers or suppliers, this feature enables you to produce multiple copies of a letter (each with a different addressee and any other details that may be required to personalize it) without laboriously having to type a copy for each recipient. Form letters use the facility known as 'mail merge'. Mail merge makes use of data sources like mailing lists or your own computer address book. The machine will automatically insert into the form letter the relevant data from the mailing list, producing a personalized copy for each person or company on the list.

Some tips

The following tips are valid for Word 97 and Word 2000:

You can let Word **check your spelling and grammar** as you write:

- Click on ABC on the standard toolbar; or click on Tools on the menu bar, then Spelling and Grammar; or simply press F7.
- On the Spelling and Grammar dialogue box, click on Options.
- Click on Check spelling as you type and/or Check Grammar as you type.
- Click on OK.
- A red wavy line will now appear under a word whose spelling is doubtful. Right-click on the wavy line to get a shortcut menu allowing you to accept Word's suggestion by clicking on it or to add the word you typed to the checking dictionary. Similarly, a green wavy line will appear under grammatical queries.

If you find the wavy lines distracting:

- Proceed as above, but click on Check spelling as you type and/or Check grammar as you type so that the tick is removed.
- You can then check the whole text after you have written it by clicking on ABC on the standard toolbar; or by clicking on Tools on the menu bar, then Spelling and Grammar; or simply by pressing F7.

> *Usage*
>
> Be careful when using spellcheck! If you have used the wrong word, but have spelt it correctly, the spellcheck will not pick it up. Particular care should be taken with words whose spellings are frequently confused, like *practise* and *practice*, *affect* and *effect*, *dependant* and *dependent*. Spellcheckers may only recognize a limited number of proper names, or they may be stumped by technical or scientific terms.

You can **stop the spellcheck** from operating in a passage containing specialized terminology (where it would query too many spellings), while keeping it for the rest of the text:

- Highlight the passage in question.
- Click on Tools on the menu bar, then Language, then Set Language.
- Choose No Proofing in the dialogue box.
- Click on OK.

You can use the **thesaurus** function to find a synonym to replace a word you have used too often or to find a word that you cannot quite remember but whose sense you know:

- Put your cursor on the word you want a synonym for, or type in a rough synonym for the word you cannot remember and put your cursor over this.
- Click on Tools on the menu bar, then Language, then Thesaurus; or simply press Shift + F7.
- Click on the appropriate meaning in the box on the left.
- Click on a synonym in the box on the right.
- Click on replace to insert the synonym in the text.

You can use the **Auto Text** function to generate phrases or sentences that you use frequently by typing in an abbreviation:

- Highlight the text that you want to store.
- Click on Insert on the menu bar, then AutoText, then AutoText.

- Click on the AutoCorrect tab.
- In the Replace box, type an abbreviation that is not likely to be used in any other context.
- Click on Add.
- Click on OK.

Now, whenever you type that abbreviation, the whole phrase or sentence will appear. This is particularly useful for standard phrases such as salutations or complimentary closes.

Sometimes a page break will leave a line or just a few words of a paragraph on one page and the rest of the paragraph on the other page. You can prevent this happening by **overriding page breaks**:
- Click anywhere in the paragraph that you want to keep together.
- Click on Format on the menu bar, then Paragraph.
- Click on the Line and Page Breaks tab.
- Click on Keep lines together.
- Click on OK.

You can **format paragraphs** and adjust **line spacing**:
- Click on Format on the menu bar, then Paragraph.
- Click on the Indents and Spacing tab.
- At Alignment, click on the pull-down menu to choose left, centred, right or justified alignment.
- In the Line Spacing box you can choose single, double or 1.5 line spacing.

If you want to format a paragraph which is already typed, simply highlight it and then go through the above procedure.

You can **customize** your menus and toolbars by adding commands (Save, Paste, Bold etc) to any menu or toolbar that you want:
- Click on Tools on the menu bar, then Customize, then the Commands tab.
- In the Categories dialogue box, click on the menu currently

containing the command you want. The commands available
are shown in the box on the right.

- If you want to add the command to a menu, click on the menu
  outside the box where you want to add the command.
- Choose the command from the dialogue box and drag it to the
  menu outside the box or to the toolbar where you want it to go.
- To remove a command, drag it on to the desktop.
- Click on Close.

You can **display formatting marks**, such as spaces, tabs and para
graph marks on the screen:

- Click on Tools on the menu bar, then Options.
- Click on the View tab.
- Click on the formatting marks (called nonprinting characters in
  Word 97) that you want to see on screen.
- Click on OK.

Paper sizes and envelopes

Paper

Paper sizes in the EU

Most of the paper we buy for writing, printing and photocopying is supplied in standard 'A' sizes. One of the advantages of this international standard for paper sizes – from the paper manufacturers' as well as their customers' point of view – is that each A size is half the area of the previous one, in a descending scale from A0 to A7. Thus, an A2 sheet folded and cut in half will produce two A3 sheets, an A3 sheet will produce two A4 sheets, and so on. If you are folding and cutting paper, it is advisable to use a guillotine, which will give a straight cut edge. Ragged or uneven edges will detract from the overall appearance of your letter.

A4 is the most popular size for business correspondence these days. A5 is also widely used, especially for shorter business letters and memos, and personal letters. Most office filing systems are designed to take A4 sheets, so it makes sense to stick to this size for correspondence that is likely to be kept for future reference.

Paper sizes in North America

In North America, standard sizes are different. The most commonly used size is **Letter** (8.5 × 11 inches or approx. 216 × 279mm). Other formats are **Legal** (8.5 × 14 inches or approx. 216 × 356 mm), **Executive** (7.5 × 10 inches or approx. 190 × 254 mm) and **Ledger** or **Tabloid** (11 × 17 inches or approx. 279 × 432 mm).

Paper types and weights

The general advice is: use the best quality, thickest paper you can afford.

Bond

A good quality paper that will not tear or crease easily, recommended for all types of letter and for continuation sheets.

Bank

A flimsy paper that is fine for drafts, carbon copies and file copies, but because it is more transparent and will tear easily, is not recommended for the letter itself.

Airmail

A thin paper whose light weight keeps down the cost of postage for letters sent by air.

EU PAPER SIZES

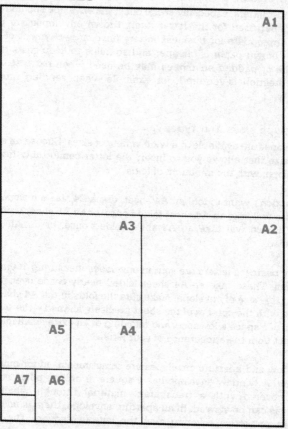

A0: 841 × 1189 mm   A3: 297 × 420 mm   A6: 105 × 148 mm
A1: 594 × 841 mm   A4: 210 × 297 mm   A7: 74 × 105 mm
A2: 420 × 594 mm   A5: 148 × 210 mm

Envelopes

For most letters, especially social ones, the envelope should match the paper used for the letter itself. Brown envelopes are really only appropriate for business letters (invoicing, payment of bills, etc) – brown paper is cheaper and so helps to keep costs down. Manila or padded envelopes may be used when extra strength or protection is required, for example when sending multiple sheets.

Envelope sizes and types

Envelopes are available in a wide variety of sizes. Choose an envelope size that allows you to insert the letter comfortably into the envelope, with the minimum of folds.

If you don't want to fold an A4 sheet, use a C4 size envelope. The C5 size will take an A4 sheet folded once, or an A5 sheet unfolded; the C6 size will take an A5 sheet folded once, or an A6 sheet unfolded.

Many business letters are sent in envelopes measuring 100mm by 220mm. These take an A4 sheet folded neatly twice over. When using this size of envelope, make sure the folds in the A4 sheet are made with the corners of the sheet precisely aligned – there is not much of a space allowance, and refolding or an extra small fold will detract from the appearance of your letter.

Window and aperture envelopes are sometimes used for business letters. A window envelope has a square or oblong panel cut out and covered with a transparent material through which the address can be viewed. In an aperture envelope, there is no transparent protective covering over the cut-out section. The letter inside must be folded and inserted correctly so that the address of the recipient appears in the correct position under the window or aperture.

Aerogrammes are specially printed sheets that function as both writing paper and envelope, with the postage pre-paid for airmail. Guide marks are printed on the sheet indicating how it should be folded before sealing.

Index

425943